Stratford Library Association
2203 Main Street
Stratford, CT 06615
203-385-4160

COMPACT *Research*

Panic
Disorder

Diseases and Disorders

ReferencePoint
Press®

San Diego, CA

Other books in the Compact Research Diseases and Disorders set:

Acne and Skin Disorders
ADHA
Anxiety Disorders
Bipolar Disorders
Bulimia
Chronic Fatigue Syndrome
Depressive Disorders
Fetal Alcohol Disorder
Food-Borne Illness
Impulse Control Disorders
Mood Disorders
Obsessive-Compulsive Disorder
Personality Disorders
Self-Injury Disorder
Sports Injuries

*For a complete list of titles please visit www.referencepointpress.com.

Panic Disorder

Peggy J. Parks

Diseases and Disorders

ReferencePoint Press®

San Diego, CA

© 2013 ReferencePoint Press, Inc.
Printed in the United States

For more information, contact:
ReferencePoint Press, Inc.
PO Box 27779
San Diego, CA 92198
www.ReferencePointPress.com

Picture credits:
Cover: Dreamstime and iStockphoto.com
Maury Aaseng: 33–35, 47–48, 59–61, 73–74
Thinkstock.com: 12, 15

LIBRARY OF CONGRESS CATALOGING-IN-PUBLICATION DATA

Parks, Peggy J., 1951–
   Panic disorder / by Peggy J. Parks.
      p. cm. -- (Compact Research series)
   Audience: Grade 9 to 12.
   Includes bibliographical references and index.
   ISBN 978-1-60152-488-1 (hardback) -- ISBN 1-60152-488-9 (hardback) 1. Panic disorders.
2. Panic disorders--Treatment. 3. Panic attacks. 4. Panic attacks--Treatment. I. Title.
   RC535.P37   2013
   616.85′223--dc23
                                                                            2012027699

Contents

Foreword   6

Panic Disorder at a Glance   8

Overview   10

What Is Panic Disorder?   22
    Primary Source Quotes   29
    Facts and Illustrations   32

What Causes Panic Disorder?   36
    Primary Source Quotes   43
    Facts and Illustrations   46

What Are the Effects of Panic Disorder?   49
    Primary Source Quotes   55
    Facts and Illustrations   58

Can People Overcome Panic Disorder?   62
    Primary Source Quotes   69
    Facts and Illustrations   72

Key People and Advocacy Groups   76

Chronology   78

Related Organizations   80

For Further Research   84

Source Notes   86

List of Illustrations   89

Index   90

About the Author   96

Foreword

A s modern civilization continues to evolve, its ability to create, store, distribute, and access information expands exponentially. The explosion of information from all media continues to increase at a phenomenal rate. By 2020 some experts predict the worldwide information base will double every seventy-three days. While access to diverse sources of information and perspectives is paramount to any democratic society, information alone cannot help people gain knowledge and understanding. Information must be organized and presented clearly and succinctly in order to be understood. The challenge in the digital age becomes not the creation of information, but how best to sort, organize, enhance, and present information.

ReferencePoint Press developed the *Compact Research* series with this challenge of the information age in mind. More than any other subject area today, researching current issues can yield vast, diverse, and unqualified information that can be intimidating and overwhelming for even the most advanced and motivated researcher. The *Compact Research* series offers a compact, relevant, intelligent, and conveniently organized collection of information covering a variety of current topics ranging from illegal immigration and deforestation to diseases such as anorexia and meningitis.

The series focuses on three types of information: objective single-author narratives, opinion-based primary source quotations, and facts and statistics. The clearly written objective narratives provide context and reliable background information. Primary source quotes are carefully selected and cited, exposing the reader to differing points of view, and facts and statistics sections aid the reader in evaluating perspectives. Presenting these key types of information creates a richer, more balanced learning experience.

For better understanding and convenience, the series enhances information by organizing it into narrower topics and adding design features that make it easy for a reader to identify desired content. For example, in *Compact Research: Illegal Immigration*, a chapter covering the economic impact of illegal immigration has an objective narrative explaining the various ways the economy is impacted, a balanced section of numerous primary source quotes on the topic, followed by facts and full-color illustrations to encourage evaluation of contrasting perspectives.

The ancient Roman philosopher Lucius Annaeus Seneca wrote, "It is quality rather than quantity that matters." More than just a collection of content, the *Compact Research* series is simply committed to creating, finding, organizing, and presenting the most relevant and appropriate amount of information on a current topic in a user-friendly style that invites, intrigues, and fosters understanding.

Panic Disorder at a Glance

Panic Disorder Defined

One of the anxiety disorders, panic disorder revolves around intense fear that leads to terrifying episodes known as panic attacks that can strike at any time.

Panic Attacks

In addition to fear and dread, panic attacks involve physical symptoms such as racing or pounding heartbeat, shortness of breath, chest pain, trembling, sweating, chills, and dizziness.

Prevalence

The National Institute of Mental Health (NIMH) estimates that 6 million Americans suffer from panic disorder. It is most common among young adults, but people of any age can develop it.

Combination of Causes

A specific cause for panic disorder is unknown, although a number of contributing factors have been identified, including heredity, family environment, and brain chemistry.

Panic Triggers

Extreme stress is known to trigger panic attacks in people with panic disorder. Anxiety about having another attack can also be a trigger.

Effects on Sufferers

Panic disorder can have a severely negative effect on a sufferer's quality of life. Alcohol and drug abuse are common among panic disorder patients, as is the development of one or more phobias.

Diagnosis

Criteria include recurrent panic attacks, concern about having attacks, fear over the consequences of panic attacks, and changes in behavior related to the attacks.

Treatment Options

Treatment plans vary from patient to patient but typically include a combination of medications and one or more types of therapy.

Overcoming Panic Disorder

Treatments can be very effective in helping people overcome panic disorder, but most sufferers never seek professional help.

Overview

A panic attack involves such a high level of anxiety that the person affected feels as if he or she can't breathe, is having a heart attack, going insane, or losing control.”

— David L. Ginsberg, clinical associate professor and medical director of clinical affairs in the Department of Psychiatry at New York University.

“**All sorts of people can have panic disorders. Men, women, children, business executives, and yes, Hollywood stars.**”

— Julie Stevenson and Raymond Le Blanc, authors of *Understanding and Overcoming Anxiety and Panic Attacks*.

Sara Benincasa is a comedian and radio personality from New Jersey who is known for her brash style of humor. Because she is a performer who often cracks jokes at her own expense, it may seem hard to believe that much of her life has been dominated by fear. From the time she was ten years old, Benincasa suffered from severe panic attacks. "I'd feel a sudden onset of terror and nausea," she says, "accompanied by a pounding heart and a throbbing skull. Sometimes my arms would start to tingle. 'I'm sick!' I'd cry, and I'd go into the bathroom at home or at school and try to throw up." By the time Benincasa was fifteen she was having panic attacks on a regular basis and started changing her routines in an attempt to prevent them. She writes: "I learned to avoid places that I couldn't easily escape. I made excuses to get out of school trips. I did everything I could to avoid riding the bus, including feigning all kinds of maladies."[1]

Now in her twenties, Benincasa has undergone treatment for panic disorder and has made excellent progress in overcoming it. As far as she has come, however, she is not completely free from panic attacks and still gets frightened when she has one. "I'm a comedian," she says, "and I've made fun of my own panic attacks so many times in front of so many people that I'm always surprised by the way the attacks still scare the crap out of me."[2]

What Is Panic Disorder?

Fear is a normal human emotion, as well as an essential one. If people never felt afraid, they would be oblivious to threats and could easily find themselves in danger. But the type of fear that plagues people with panic disorder is intense to the point of being unbearable and leads to panic attacks that the sufferer feels powerless to stop. These attacks can happen anywhere, whether someone is sitting in a classroom, surfing the Internet, shopping at the mall, or just walking down the street. College professor and historian Michael E. Brooks recalls two frightening occasions when he had panic attacks while driving, as he writes: "One time the attack was so severe that I could not drive across a mile-long section of elevated highway and I parked on the shoulder until it passed, while the other time I managed to grit my teeth and drive the remaining two miles back to my house."[3]

> " The type of fear that plagues people with panic disorder is intense to the point of being unbearable and leads to panic attacks that the sufferer feels powerless to stop. "

Panic disorder is one of the anxiety disorders, a group of mental conditions that includes obsessive-compulsive disorder, phobias, and post-traumatic stress disorder (PTSD). Each of these disorders has its own unique characteristics, but the one trait they share is excessive, irrational fear and dread. What distinguishes panic disorder from other anxiety disorders is that panic attacks can develop for no apparent reason, rather than being rooted in the fear of a particular object or situation.

Panic Attack Symptoms

The hallmark of a panic attack is a sudden rush of intense fear that strikes without warning. People who witness someone having a panic attack are often shocked that the person seemed fine one minute and was con-

Panic disorder can produce sudden, paralyzing fear in a crowded public setting such as a shopping mall (pictured) or in the privacy of one's own home. These panic attacks can be linked to fear of a particular object or situation, but they can also occur without any apparent cause or warning.

sumed with panic the next—and that confusion is shared by panic disorder sufferers. They, too, are caught off-guard by the panic that suddenly sweeps over them, as one man in his mid-twenties describes: "My first panic attack threw me for a loop when I was 21. I had no idea what was happening to me. One moment I was standing there talking to my dad, and the next I'm rushing to sit down on the couch and contemplating calling 911. The world was spinning, my heart was racing, and I felt I was going to die right there."[4]

A racing or pounding heartbeat (known as palpitations) is one of the most common physical symptoms associated with panic attacks. This is often accompanied by chest pain and shortness of breath, which can frighten sufferers into believing that they are having a heart attack. An article on the mental health website Psych Central explains:

> When a panic attack strikes, most likely your heart pounds and you may feel sweaty, weak, faint, or dizzy. Your hands may tingle or feel numb, and you might feel flushed or chilled. You may have chest pain or smothering sensations, a sense of unreality, or fear of impending doom or loss of control. You may genuinely believe you're having a heart attack or stroke, losing your mind, or on the verge of death.[5]

The Urge to Escape

Many people with panic disorder say that when they have panic attacks they are overcome by an irresistible urge to take off running, as though they can somehow escape from their fear. Sufferers report fleeing from grounded airplanes, subways, boats, and theaters, as well as scores of other places. One of psychiatrist Carol W. Berman's patients was riding a city bus when she had a panic attack. When the bus stopped she jumped off and started running. She ended up breaking her ankle. Says Berman: "The feelings usually involve the belief that the person will be trapped in some small space, and experience the horrible fear of a panic attack. Running away doesn't stop the actual symptoms of the panic attack, but people distract themselves by running."[6]

Military veteran Jason D. Cooper followed his instinct to flee—and it nearly cost him his life. Cooper is a former sniper with the US Marine

Corps who suffers from both PTSD and panic disorder. In February 2012 he was involved in a minor traffic accident while driving along a highway in Oregon's Cascade Mountains. After rear-ending the car in front of him, Cooper panicked, jumped out of his vehicle, and fled into the woods. He was dressed in light summer clothing and wore only sandals on his feet, so national park officials feared that he might die of exposure in the deep snow and bitterly cold temperatures. Rescuers found him nearly two days later, huddled beneath pine boughs and in surprisingly good shape. Says Dave Randall, an Oregon State Police trooper who helped with the rescue: "I found out that he had panic attacks during stressful situations and sometimes just had to run away."[7]

> As horrible as panic attacks can be for anyone who is plagued by them, an occasional attack does not necessarily mean the person has panic disorder.

Connected but Different

As horrible as panic attacks can be for anyone who is plagued by them, an occasional attack does not necessarily mean the person has panic disorder. Some people may have one panic attack and never experience another, or have them only in certain situations. For instance, someone with a phobia about spiders might have a panic attack if one crawls across a hand or foot, and an individual who is claustrophobic may have an attack when riding on a packed elevator. Or panic attacks may be triggered by excessive worry, as clinical psychologist Charles H. Elliott explains: "Many people experience episodes of mild to moderate panic here and there—a few of the common triggers for such episodes include looming deadlines, upcoming parties, and presentations to work groups. However, some people experience panic at a much more intense level, to the point that they actually develop a full blown Panic Disorder."[8]

People who suffer from panic disorder are plagued by recurrent panic attacks, even having them multiple times a day. In her book *100 Questions & Answers About Panic Disorder*, Berman discusses the worst case of panic disorder she has ever seen in her professional career. The woman,

Many people have a fear of spiders or of public speaking, and some even freeze up at the sight of a spider or at the notion of speaking before a group. But having these fears is not the same as suffering from the debilitating attacks that are experienced by those with panic disorder.

who was a high school teacher, suffered from panic attacks at least twenty times per day over a period of two years. "She would hardly finish one attack before another one would start," says Berman. "They were overwhelming, relentless attacks accompanied by a racing heart, shortness of breath, and a fear of dying or going crazy."[9]

Millions Affected

Anxiety disorders collectively represent the most common form of mental illness in the United States. According to the NIMH, an estimated 40 million adults in the United States suffer from one or more anxiety disorder, with panic disorder affecting about 6 million. Symptoms usually develop during the late teenage years or early adulthood, but males and females of any age can suffer from panic disorder. A May 2012 article in the publication *Assisted Living Today* explains: "Panic attacks are not altogether uncommon in the elderly. Panic attacks in the elderly tend to be linked with the life changes and challenges that accompany the age group."[10]

> **Many who suffer from panic disorder are caught in a vicious cycle of fear.**

Although the reason is not well understood, panic disorder is about twice as common among women as men. Berman says that the disorder "is often thought of as a 'female problem' that men are reluctant to admit they have." Many men do suffer from panic disorder, however, as Berman writes: "Men may . . . report panic attacks less frequently and try to 'tough it out' by drinking or drugging. One of my patients didn't realize he had panic attacks until he stopped his daily use of marijuana. Then he started having them three times a week."[11]

Young Sufferers

Panic disorder is most common among young adults, but children can develop it, too. According to a 2010 paper by the psychiatric staff at Massachusetts General Hospital, panic disorder in children may be mistaken for another condition, as they tend to complain about physical symptoms that accompany panic attacks rather than the psychological symptoms. The Massachusetts General group writes: "Sometimes children having a panic attack incorrectly explain their symptoms as a response to an external trigger (for example, 'It started when I saw that dog'). These children, particularly if they are very young, may not be able to articulate the intense fears they experience during a panic attack."[12]

The Canadian support group Anxiety BC tells the story of an eleven-year-old girl named Andrea, who had her first panic attack just before taking a test at school. She was suffering from chest pain and breathing problems, so her teacher sent her to the school nurse. Following that experience, Andrea had several more panic attacks at school, as well as one while she was out for dinner with her family. These attacks have frightened her so much that she has missed school and refuses to eat in restaurants out of fear that she will have more panic attacks. Such reactions are typical of young panic disorder sufferers, as Anxiety BC explains: "Children and teens may stop participating in activities that they think could lead to panic attacks, such as driving through a tunnel, entering crowded places, or participating in physical activities (for example, running). They may also refuse to attend school or participate in hobbies and interests."[13]

> " In an attempt to cope with the near-constant fear of panic disorder, many sufferers adopt habits that are harmful, such as abusing alcohol and smoking. "

What Causes Panic Disorder?

As with all anxiety disorders (and mental illnesses in general), no one knows exactly what causes panic disorder. Years of research have yielded many different theories, as the American Psychological Association writes: "There may be a genetic predisposition to anxiety disorders; some sufferers report that a family member has or had a panic disorder or some other emotional disorder such as depression. . . . Panic Disorder could also be due to a biological malfunction, although a specific biological marker has yet to be identified."[14]

The American Psychological Association's mention of genetics is significant because panic disorder tends to run in families. According to the National Institutes of Health, studies have shown that if one identical twin has panic disorder, the other twin will also develop the condition 40 percent of the time. Such findings do not prove that panic disorder is hereditary, however, since most people who are genetically predisposed never develop the disorder. Thus, the prevailing scientific belief is that multiple causes are involved, with panic disorder resulting from a complex interaction of biological and environmental factors.

Terrorized by Fear

Many who suffer from panic disorder are caught in a vicious cycle of fear. They become so consumed with dread over when the next panic attack will strike that it fuels their fear, and the more frightened they become the more attacks they have. Over time, their anxiety grows so intense that it triggers more panic attacks, which is one of the most difficult, disabling effects of panic disorder. As one sufferer explains: "The more attacks I had, the more afraid I got. I was always living in fear. I didn't know when I might have another attack. I became so afraid that I didn't want to leave my house."[15]

Developing a fear of leaving home is not uncommon among people with panic disorder. Because of how deeply afraid they are of having panic attacks, they come to believe that the only place they will be safe is behind locked doors. These people have developed agoraphobia, which is a devastating, crippling anxiety disorder. Although the literal translation of the word is "fear of open spaces," those who suffer from agoraphobia are haunted by innumerable fears, as psychiatrist David L. Ginsberg writes:

> People with agoraphobia often avoid being out alone, going to supermarkets, traveling in trains or airplanes, crossing bridges, climbing to heights, going through tunnels, crossing open fields, and riding in elevators. Agoraphobia takes a toll not only on those afflicted, but on their friends and loved ones, who often are called upon to accompany them on everyday tasks and errands.[16]

What Are the Effects of Panic Disorder?

People who are plagued by repeated panic attacks and have no idea when the next one will strike suffer from a great deal of emotional anguish. It can be terribly frustrating to have no control over the attacks or what might trigger them, which inevitably creates feelings of helplessness. According to the Mayo Clinic, the complications of panic disorder can affect every area of a sufferer's life, as the group writes: "You may be so afraid of having more panic attacks that you live in a constant state of fear, ruining your quality of life."[17]

In an attempt to cope with the near-constant fear of panic disorder, many sufferers adopt habits that are harmful, such as abusing alcohol and smoking. This was a major finding of a study that was published in the February 1, 2011, issue of the *Journal of Cognitive Psychotherapy*. University of Houston researcher Peter J. Norton and colleagues investigated the lifestyle habits of 489 people, of whom 107 reported a history of panic attacks. Within that group, alcohol abuse was twice as prevalent and habitual smoking was three times more prevalent than among participants with no history of panic attacks. The study authors write: "Results of the current study support that, consistent with the existing literature . . . individuals experiencing panic attacks show significantly higher rates of smoking, alcohol use, and hazardous or harmful alcohol use."[18]

> " Because people with panic disorder are often ashamed of their panic attacks, most never seek professional help. They would rather suffer in silence than risk being told their problem is imagined, or worse, that they are crazy. "

How Panic Disorder Is Diagnosed

When an individual seeks medical attention for recurring panic attacks, he or she will first have a complete physical examination and a series of blood tests. These procedures help doctors rule out any medical conditions that might be causing the attacks, such as problems with the heart or thyroid. The physician is also likely to ask questions about alcohol and drugs, as symptoms of substance abuse can mimic those of panic attacks.

If tests find no underlying medical conditions, the next step is a mental health evaluation. This often involves a team of professionals such as psychiatrists, psychologists, and/or licensed therapists who ask questions and use specific testing methods to analyze the patient's symptoms. A diagnosis of panic disorder must meet criteria listed in the American Psychiatric Association's *Diagnostic and Statistical Manual of Mental Disorders*, which is often called the "bible" of mental illnesses. Panic disorder criteria include recurrent, unexpected panic attacks for more than a month combined with at least one of the following: persistent concern about having additional attacks, worry about the consequences of panic attacks (such as losing control or "going crazy"), and a significant change in behavior as a result of the attacks.

Can People Overcome Panic Disorder?

Because people with panic disorder are often ashamed of their panic attacks, most never seek professional help. They would rather suffer in silence than risk being told their problem is imagined or, worse, that they are crazy. Also, many with panic disorder convince themselves that there is no hope for them, as the Bridges to Recovery group explains: "Perhaps one reason that people do not seek treatment for their panic disorder is the fear that they can never be completely cured. With this pessimistic point of view, they forgo treatment, feeling that they are a hopeless case. In reality, however, panic disorder can be managed so that patients experience few—if any—symptoms of the disorder."[19]

Although treatment plans vary from patient to patient, these generally include one or more types of psychotherapy, antianxiety medications, or both. One type of therapy that is often used for people with panic disorder is cognitive behavioral therapy (CBT), which the NIMH says "teaches a person different ways of thinking, behaving, and reacting to situations that help him or her feel less anxious and fearful."[20] CBT therapists help the patient identify negative thought patterns, and the behaviors that result from them, in order to get at the root cause of the panic attacks. Once dysfunctional thoughts are identified, the patient is taught to pay attention to why the thoughts develop, and he or she learns how to address them at an early stage. Over time, patients can use these skills to head off panic attacks before they strike.

Fear, Frustration, and Hope

Although fear is a normal human emotion, the paralyzing fear that is characteristic of panic disorder is anything but normal. Panic attacks can strike without warning, at any time of the day or night, and are unpredictable as well as terrifying for anyone who has them. Many sufferers become so terrified about when the next attack might strike that they confine themselves to their homes. Yet there is hope for these people, because with the right treatment many patients overcome panic disorder and go on to live happy, healthy lives. Benincasa is one of them, as she has made great strides in overcoming her panic disorder. In reference to the panic attacks that once plagued her, she writes: "They don't put a stop to my entire life anymore. . . . Odd as it sounds, I no longer panic about my panic."[21]

What Is
Panic Disorder?

66Panic attacks were once dismissed as nerves or stress, but they're now recognized as a real medical condition.99

—Mayo Clinic, a world-renowned medical facility headquartered in Rochester, Minnesota.

66A full-blown panic attack is not just a strong feeling of anxiety but rather an explosion of terror that the brain reserves for only the most horrifying events.99

—Jason Eric Schiffman, chief resident psychiatrist at the University of California–Los Angeles Anxiety Disorders Program.

Scientific exploration of human anxiety traces back thousands of years to writings by the Greek physician Hippocrates. The concept of panic also originated in Greece—but it is not rooted in science. Rather, it is a product of ancient mythology and the story of a god known as Pan. According to legend, Pan roamed the wilderness areas of Greece and concealed himself from travelers by hiding behind thick bushes. As unsuspecting passersby neared his hiding place, Pan planted seeds of apprehension in their minds by making rustling noises. When they hurried away, as Pan always knew they would, he rushed ahead to intercept them at the next dark path.

Pan found this game to be a source of amusement and kept it up as his victims grew more and more fearful. Ronald Hoffman, a physician, author, and radio host from New York City, writes:

> The traveler would begin to breathe heavily, and his heart
> would begin to pound, and the sounds of his own quick-

ening footsteps would be magnified in the stillness of the forest to resemble those of a pursuing wild animal. One more rustle of the bushes from Pan and the traveler would be hurtling as fast as he could run along the dark and narrow forest path. . . . Never would the unsuspecting traveler re-enter the forest without experiencing a wave of apprehension. Thus did the term panic originate.[22]

Early Observations

The earliest known scientific reference to panic attacks was by the great philosopher Plato, who was born in Athens, Greece, in 429 BC. In his book titled *Timaeus*, Plato discussed the prevalence of panic among young women, since he had observed that they were the most typical sufferers. He theorized that if women waited too long after puberty to get pregnant, the womb became "distressed and sorely disturbed," leading to symptoms such as poor respiration and severe shortness of breath, which "brings the sufferer into the extremist anguish and provokes all the manner of diseases besides."[23] Medical scholars later credited Plato with being the first to identify panic attack symptoms and acknowledged the accuracy of his belief that the attacks were most common among young women of childbearing age.

More than two thousand years after Plato's book was written, the Austrian neurologist Sigmund Freud documented his own observations of panic disorder. As had Plato before him, Freud noted that panic attacks involved the inability to get one's breath (known as dyspnea), which today is a known characteristic of panic attacks. In a letter written to a colleague during the late nineteenth century, Freud described a panic attack as reported by one of his female patients, whom he referred to as suffering from hysteria. The patient noted: "I woke up at 2:30 am with hot flashes. My whole body felt like it was burning up, my neck and hair were wet with sweat. My skin felt prickly; if I had hair on my back, it would have been standing up. I felt like I couldn't

> " The earliest known scientific reference to panic attacks was by the great philosopher Plato. "

breathe . . . like I was being burned alive. It was the worst terror I had ever experienced."[24]

According to Donald F. Klein, a Columbia University psychiatrist and noted expert on panic disorder, the patient's reference to having the panic attack at night was a strong indication that she suffered from panic disorder, rather than a different type of anxiety. In a 1996 paper about early studies of panic attacks, Klein referred to Freud's "clinical astuteness" in understanding how panic disorder differed from other conditions; specifically his correct assessment of nighttime panic attacks. Klein wrote: "Nocturnal panic attacks are peculiar to panic disorder—social phobics and obsessive compulsives do not get them, and they occur in no other anxiety disorder."[25]

Klein also noted Freud's awareness that dyspnea was unique to panic disorder, calling it "one of the cardinal features of the spontaneous attack in panic disorder." This, said Klein, was different from other anxiety disorders in which dyspnea was not a typical symptom. He explained: "For instance, social phobia—performance anxiety, public speaking anxiety— is classically marked by palpitations, sweating, and trembling; i.e., fear but not dyspnea."[26]

Cued Versus Uncued Attacks

The primary characteristic of panic disorder is recurrent panic attacks that strike suddenly and unexpectedly. Thus, the American Psychiatric Association refers to these as unexpected (or uncued) panic attacks, meaning that they happen in the absence of any obvious cause or trigger. Psychiatrist Carol W. Berman describes such an attack: "You are sitting at your work desk minding your own business when out of the blue, a dreadful feeling rises out of your chest into your throat. Your heart is racing. You can't breathe. You sweat, shake, and get dizzy. As you clutch your chair to steady yourself, you think, 'What's going on? Am I going crazy?'"[27] According to Berman, unexpected panic attacks are especially upsetting for sufferers. Because the attacks have no known trigger, those who suffer from them have no way to protect themselves by avoiding specific objects or situations.

Although patients must have panic attacks of the unexpected type to be diagnosed with panic disorder, they may also suffer from two other types of panic attacks. These are triggered by known fears and are categorized by the American Psychiatric Association as situationally bound and situationally predisposed panic attacks. The former, which are also called cued panic attacks, often affect panic disorder patients who suffer from phobias such as fear of heights, confined places, flying in airplanes, and speaking in front of audiences. Los Angeles psychiatrist Jason Eric Schiffman draws a contrast between cued and uncued panic attacks: "Someone with a strong fear of public speaking might have a situational panic attack before having to give a speech to a large audience, while someone with unexpected panic attacks would have a difficult time identifying why the panic attack occurred."[28]

> **The primary characteristic of panic disorder is recurrent panic attacks that strike suddenly and unexpectedly. Thus, the American Psychiatric Association refers to these as unexpected (or uncued) panic attacks.**

Situationally predisposed panic attacks also involve known fears. They are slightly different from cued attacks, though, because they may or may not occur when a panic disorder sufferer is exposed to a particular trigger. For instance, someone who has had panic attacks while driving will not necessarily have an attack every time he or she is behind the wheel of a car. Another example is an individual who suffers from acrophobia (fear of heights) being on the thirtieth floor of a highrise apartment building, as Berman writes: "It is likely that this person will get a panic attack if someone forces her out on the terrace and she looks down, but she may not get a panic attack just by being in the apartment. It isn't certain that a panic attack will happen every time."[29]

Panic Disorder Plus

Mental health experts say that it is common for people with panic disorder to suffer from coexisting medical and/or psychological illnesses, which is known as comorbidity. Conditions that often accompany panic disorder include agoraphobia; restless leg syndrome, in which individuals feel the urge to keep moving their legs to stop unpleasant sensations;

major depression; chronic fatigue; and cardiovascular disorders, which affect the heart and blood vessels.

A number of studies have shown that recurrent headaches commonly affect people with panic disorder. These may include tension headaches, which involve tightening of the muscles in the head, neck, and shoulders that leads to pain throughout the head; and migraine headaches, which are much more severe and may last from a few hours to several days. Those who suffer from migraines typically feel strong pressure and pain behind one or both eyes; become acutely sensitive to sounds, smells, and/or light; may experience blurred vision and even temporary loss of eyesight; and often suffer from nausea and vomiting.

> **A number of studies have shown that recurrent headaches commonly affect people with panic disorder.**

Jeff Tweedy, who is lead singer, songwriter, and guitarist of the Chicago-based rock band Wilco, was diagnosed with both panic disorder and migraine headaches. Tweedy has had panic attacks since he was a teenager and says he cannot remember a time in his life when he did not suffer from severe headaches. Because he is affected by both conditions, he can see definite parallels between them, saying that "the arc of a migraine is very similar to some of the traits of panic disorder." He explains:

> One of the things that happens a lot with panic disorder is that you'll have an actual panic attack and for weeks or months after that you'll have a fear of a panic attack that can heighten your anxiety and heighten your stress levels to the point where you end up having another panic attack. To me those things mirror each other. Migraines would add stress to my life in a way that would contribute to the next headache and it would begin a cycle that would be hard to stop. So I would have periods where I would have a migraine very frequently—every other day or twice a week—for months.[30]

An Eye-Opening Study

For as long as panic disorder has been studied, the unpredictability of panic attacks has remained perplexing to scientists—and frustrating for sufferers. What makes panic disorder especially difficult is knowing that an attack can occur suddenly and for no obvious reason. Says Alicia E. Meuret, a psychologist at Southern Methodist University in Dallas, Texas: "In an unexpected panic attack, the patient reports the attack to occur out-of-the-blue. They would say they were sitting watching TV when they were suddenly hit by a rush of symptoms, and there wasn't anything that made it predictable."[31] That unpredictability may eventually disappear, however, because of a groundbreaking study that was published in July 2011. A team of researchers led by Meuret discovered that panic attacks are foreshadowed by subtle physiological signals up to an hour before the attacks occur.

Forty-three panic disorder patients were involved in the study. All participants were outfitted with an array of electrodes and sensors that were attached to various parts of their bodies and to a monitoring device that was toted in a waist pack. The equipment measured physiological data such as body temperature, respiration (how deep, fast, or irregularly they were breathing), cardiac activity, and evidence of sweating. A panic button was mounted on each pack, and participants were instructed to press it if they had a panic attack and then record their symptoms in a journal. As the participants went about their normal daily activities, the research team monitored them around the clock. By the end of the project, they had collected nearly two thousand hours of data, including data captured before, during, and after thirteen recorded panic attacks.

> **For as long as panic disorder has been studied, the unpredictability of panic attacks has remained perplexing to scientists—and frustrating for sufferers.**

When Meuret and her colleagues analyzed the information, they found that distinct physiological changes were present in the panic attack sufferers up to sixty minutes before the attacks occurred. "The results were just amazing," says Meuret. "We found that in this hour preceding naturally occurring panic attacks, there was a lot of physiological instability. These significant physiological instabilities were not present during other times when the patient wasn't about to have a panic attack." Participants reported that they did not feel the changes, nor did they have any idea that a panic attack was going to strike. Meuret explains: "The changes don't seem to enter the patient's awareness. What they report is what happens at the end of the 60 minutes—that they're having an out-of-the-blue panic attack with a lot of intense physical sensations."[32]

The researchers were enthusiastic about the study results and what they could potentially mean for patients. According to Meuret, the findings are significant not only for panic disorder but also for other medical conditions with symptoms that occur suddenly, such as seizures and strokes. She explains: "I think this method and study will ultimately help detect what's going on before these unexpected events and help determine how to prevent them. If we know what's happening before the event, it's easier to treat it."[33]

Yesterday, Today, and Tomorrow

Panic disorder has been a topic of interest for scholars and scientists dating back to Plato's observations over two thousand years ago. As the centuries have passed, a great deal has been learned about the disorder, yet in many ways it remains a mystery. Research continues to yield new findings, and as more studies are conducted, scientific understanding will continue to grow. For now, however, panic disorder is considered to be a condition for which there are more questions than answers.

What Is Panic Disorder?

66 **Panic disorder has been recognized in various forms for centuries.** 99

> —Dan J. Stein, Eric Hollander, and Barbara O. Rothbaum, *Textbook of Anxiety Disorders*. Arlington, VA: American Psychiatric, 2010.

Stein is a psychiatrist from Cape Town, South Africa; Hollander is a psychiatrist from New York City; and Rothbaum is a psychiatry professor at Atlanta's Emory University.

66 **Once a person knows his condition is panic disorder, he can stop believing that he's having a heart attack or going crazy.** 99

> —Carol W. Berman, *100 Questions & Answers About Panic Disorder*. Sudbury, MA: Jones and Bartlett, 2010.

Berman is a clinical instructor of psychiatry at New York University Medical School.

66 **Panic disorder is at the 'top end' of the anxiety disorder symptom spectrum and represents the very worst physical manifestation of the disorder.** 99

> —International Association of Anxiety Management, "Panic Disorder," 2012. www.anxman.org.

The International Association of Anxiety Management is a web resource for those who suffer from panic and other anxiety disorders.

* Editor's Note: While the definition of a primary source can be narrowly or broadly defined, for the purposes of Compact Research, a primary source consists of: 1) results of original research presented by an organization or researcher; 2) eyewitness accounts of events, personal experience, or work experience; 3) first-person editorials offering pundits' opinions; 4) government officials presenting political plans and/or policies; 5) representatives of organizations presenting testimony or policy.

❝Panic attacks come like a bolt out of the blue and can end just as quickly.❞

—Anthony Komaroff, "What Is the Treatment for Panic Attacks?," Ask Doctor K., January 17, 2012. www.askdoctork.com.

Komaroff is a professor of medicine at Harvard Medical School.

❝As the panic attacks occur in more and more places, people with this disorder tend to restrict their activities until, in severe cases, they refuse to leave home.❞

—Lourie W. Reichenberg and Linda Seligman, *Selecting Effective Treatments: A Comprehensive, Systematic Guide to Treating Mental Disorders*. Hoboken, NJ: Wiley, 2012.

Reichenberg is a licensed professional counselor from Falls Church, Virginia, and Seligman (who died in 2007) was a professor emeritus of counseling and development at George Mason University.

❝Panic disorder often coexists with mood disorders, with mood symptoms potentially following the onset of panic attacks.❞

—Mohammed A. Memon, "Panic Disorder," Medscape, March 29, 2011. http://emedicine.medscape.com.

Memon is chair of the Department of Psychiatry at the Spartanburg Regional Medical Center in Spartanburg, South Carolina.

❝The key symptom of panic disorder is the persistent fear of having future panic attacks.❞

—American Psychological Association, "Answers to Your Questions About Panic Disorder," 2012. www.apa.org.

The American Psychological Association is a scientific and professional organization that represents the field of psychology in the United States.

---

66 Many people with panic disorder develop intense anxiety between episodes, worrying when and where the next one will strike. 99

—Mental Health America, "Panic Disorder," 2012. www.mentalhealthamerica.net.

Mental Health America is dedicated to helping all people live mentally healthier lives and educating the public about mental health and mental illness.

66 Panic Disorder with Agoraphobia is when an individual is fearful of having a panic attack outside of the home where escape would be difficult or where help is not available. The grocery store, driving, and being in a crowd are some examples. 99

—Jennifer L. Abel, "Panic Attacks: What ARE They?," January 3, 2011. www.anxietystlouispsychologist.com.

Abel is a clinical psychologist from Clayton, Missouri.

Facts and Illustrations

What Is Panic Disorder?

- The American Psychological Association estimates that **one out of every seventy-five** people suffers from panic disorder.

- Massachusetts General Hospital estimates that **5 percent** of adolescents suffer from panic disorder.

- According to Harvard Medical School professor of medicine Anthony Komaroff, about **5 percent** of women and **2 percent** of men have panic attacks at some point in their lives.

- The Cleveland Clinic states that about **40 percent** of panic disorder sufferers also meet the criteria for agoraphobia.

- According to a March 2011 paper by psychiatrist Mohammed A. Memon, panic disorder is found in **5 to 40 percent** of individuals with asthma and **20 percent** of people with epilepsy.

- The National Institutes of Health states that most panic attacks peak within **ten to twenty minutes**.

- According to the NIMH, about **one out of every three** people with panic disorder also suffers from agoraphobia.

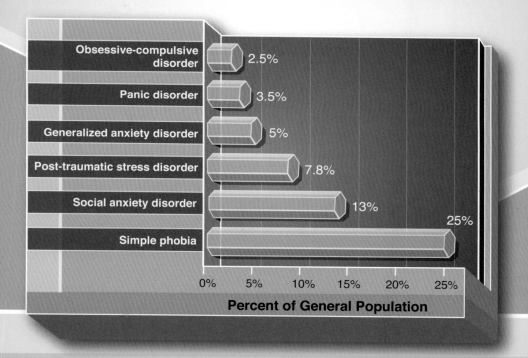

Panic Disorder Rarer than Other Anxiety Disorders

With over 40 million sufferers, anxiety disorders collectively represent one of the most common forms of mental illness in the United States. Panic disorder is, however, less common than several other forms of anxiety disorder.

Disorder	Percent
Obsessive-compulsive disorder	2.5%
Panic disorder	3.5%
Generalized anxiety disorder	5%
Post-traumatic stress disorder	7.8%
Social anxiety disorder	13%
Simple phobia	25%

Percent of General Population

Source: Jess Rowney, Teresa Hermida, and Donald Malone, "Anxiety Disorders," Cleveland Clinic, August 1, 2010. www.clevelandclinicmeded.com.

- An August 2010 paper by the Cleveland Clinic states that panic disorder has the second-lowest prevalence rate of all anxiety disorders, with **obsessive-compulsive disorder** having the lowest.

- Psychiatrist Carol W. Berman states that **women are three times** more likely to develop coexisting panic disorder and agoraphobia than men.

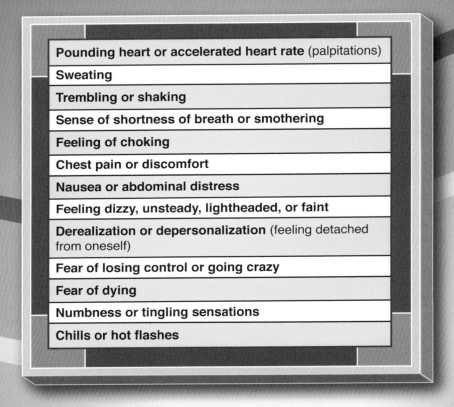

Panic Attack Symptoms

The American Psychiatric Association has established diagnostic criteria for all mental illnesses, including panic disorder. To be formally classified as a panic attack, at least four of the following symptoms must be present.

Pounding heart or accelerated heart rate (palpitations)
Sweating
Trembling or shaking
Sense of shortness of breath or smothering
Feeling of choking
Chest pain or discomfort
Nausea or abdominal distress
Feeling dizzy, unsteady, lightheaded, or faint
Derealization or depersonalization (feeling detached from oneself)
Fear of losing control or going crazy
Fear of dying
Numbness or tingling sensations
Chills or hot flashes

Source: Mohammed A. Memon, "Panic Disorder," Medscape, March 29, 2011. http://emedicine.medscape.com.

- According to the NIMH, nearly three-fourths of people with an anxiety disorder will have their first episode (such as a panic attack) **before the age of twenty-one.**

- The Anxiety Disorders Foundation states that panic disorder with agoraphobia affects about **5 percent** of the population.

An Illness of Young Adults

Although people of all ages can develop panic disorder, this graph shows that it is much more common among young adults than other anxiety disorders, some of which develop during childhood.

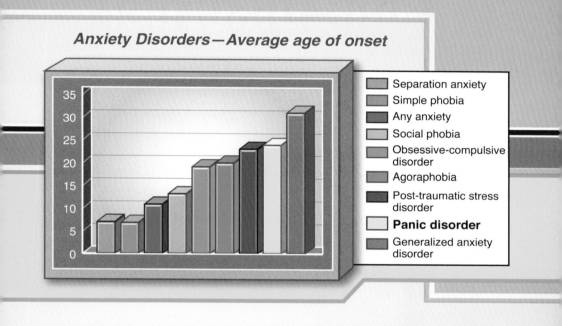

Anxiety Disorders—Average age of onset

Legend:
- Separation anxiety
- Simple phobia
- Any anxiety
- Social phobia
- Obsessive-compulsive disorder
- Agoraphobia
- Post-traumatic stress disorder
- **Panic disorder**
- Generalized anxiety disorder

Source: William R. Yates, "Anxiety Disorders," April 20, 2010. http://emedicine.medscape.com.

- A study published in January 2011 by researchers from Tokyo, Japan, found that out of fifty-four panic disorder patients, **61.1 percent** also suffered from **migraine headaches**.

What Causes Panic Disorder?

"The exact cause or causes of panic disorder are unknown and are the subject of intense scientific investigation."

—Mental Health America, an organization dedicated to helping all people live mentally healthier lives and educating the public about mental health and mental illness.

"Physical and psychological causes of panic disorder work together."

—American Psychological Association, a scientific and professional organization that represents the field of psychology in the United States.

A young woman named Brittany has battled anxiety for much of her life and developed panic disorder when she was a teenager. As a child she felt different from other kids because she was often nervous and was teased because of it. "My family labeled me a drama queen or overly sensitive," she says, "and my best friend would call me a 'scaredy cat.'"[34] Brittany's parents were divorced, and she lived with her mother, with whom she had a close, loving relationship. With her father, however, things were very different. Whenever she stayed with him, he was abusive toward her and made her feel like she could never quite measure up to his expectations. Brittany is convinced that this played a major role in her insecurities and anxiety issues, as she explains: "You could never be pretty enough, smart enough, or good enough for my father."[35]

Brittany had her first panic attack when she was fourteen years old and says it came upon her with no warning: "I just remember sitting in my bedroom and doing my homework, and all of a sudden feeling like I couldn't breathe. My heart was racing, my hands were tingling, and I was convinced I was going to die. I've never had a heart attack, but I think that is what it would feel like."[36] Brittany says that most of her panic attacks happen during what she refers to as a "nervous day," when she feels anxious and keyed up without really knowing why. Other times the attacks are like the first one, springing out of nowhere and catching her by surprise. "I can be calm one minute and feel like I am losing my mind the next," she says. "This is something I have never understood and has never been fully explained to me. But I've learned this is very common."[37]

Nature Versus Nurture

Unexpected panic attacks are indeed common for panic disorder sufferers, and that is one reason why the disorder is so perplexing. Scientists have studied it for years and are still not certain what triggers the attacks, or why some people develop panic disorder when so many others do not. Since research has shown that the disorder runs in families, this suggests a genetic basis, although whether it is hereditary is more a theory than a certainty. A widely held viewpoint among researchers is that a number of factors work together to create panic disorder, as New York therapist Mark Sichel writes:

> There are those who would make the argument that panic disorder is solely a biological phenomenon, whereas others would take the opposite stance and contend that panic is related solely to environment and developed personality traits. Most practicing psychotherapists tend to view a problem like panic disorder as being related to *both* human anatomy and human psychology.[38]

Family environment is considered to be a significant contributor to panic disorder because children can learn certain behaviors by observing their parents. Sara Benincasa has a strong family history of anxiety disorders, and she believes that her panic disorder developed largely because of what she was exposed to throughout her childhood. She writes:

> Part of my fear was a learned behavior; my dad had certain psychological issues surrounding travel, and when en route to the airport he experienced intense general anxi-

ety that sometimes led to panic attacks and other times led to bouts of strong anger. I learned to hate airports, bus terminals, and train stations, because they made my dad scared or they made him mean. My mother attempted to control every last detail of every trip in order to stave off my father's panic or anger, and so her behavior, too, was fraught with anxiety.[39]

The Stress Factor

Scientists have long suspected that stress plays a key role in the development of panic disorder. Innumerable situations and events can cause people stress, especially major life changes such as the birth of a child, divorce or separation, loss of employment, the illness or death of a loved one, and traumatic occurrences such as a serious accident or violent crime. Says the American Psychological Association: "Some researchers liken the 'life stressor' to a thermostat; that is, when stresses lower your resistance, the underlying physical predisposition kicks in and triggers an attack."[40]

> **Family environment is considered to be a significant contributor to panic disorder because children can learn certain behaviors by observing their parents.**

Examining the connection between stress and panic disorder was the focus of a study by researchers from Brown University's Alpert Medical School in Providence, Rhode Island. Over four hundred people with panic disorder were involved in the study, which was published in June 2011. The research team, led by psychiatrist Ethan Moitra, set out to determine the ways in which stressful life events affected the severity of panic attacks. The participants were asked detailed questions about stressors in their lives, including those involving relationships with family and friends, residence, employment, school, and health. They were also asked about their anxiety in connection with these experiences and were then monitored for a period before and after the events occurred.

Prior to the study the research team assumed that those who went through a stressful situation would show the effects right away by having panic attacks, but that did not happen. Rather than affecting people before or immediately after events, panic steadily worsened over the following three months. According to Moitra, this shows that stress can build up over time and result in more severe panic attacks among panic disorder sufferers. He says it is good information for physicians to know when treating patients with panic disorder, as he explains:

> What this study tells clinicians is that they need to be aware that, although people may have an immediate reaction, be vigilant in keeping track of how patients are doing over the next few months after the event, and perhaps even longer. . . . After these bad things happen and the dust settles, don't assume the person is going to be okay and back to what their baseline was. They're actually at risk for getting even worse.[41]

Clues Within the Brain

Through years of research, scientists have become convinced that the brain holds the answers to many questions about how and why panic disorder develops. The most powerful, complex organ in the human body, the brain performs like a master command and control center, responsible for everything from intelligence, imagination, emotions, and memory, to body movements and behavior. The key to brain function is its intricate network of cells known as neurons, which are constantly sending messages to each other via rapid-fire electrical signals. This ongoing communication is facilitated by chemicals known as neurotransmitters, whose function is to transfer signals from one neuron to another across tiny gaps known as synapses. Sichel explains: "Just like the various instant messaging systems on our computers, the neurotransmitters transfer information from one part of the brain to the other."[42]

> "Through years of research, scientists have become convinced that the brain holds the answers to many questions about how and why panic disorder develops."

Scientists believe that hundreds of neurotransmitters are produced by the brain, and they have identified several that likely contribute to panic disorder. These include serotonin, which helps regulate a variety of body functions as well as emotions, feelings, and mood; dopamine, which influences emotions, feelings of pleasure and reward, and body movement; and epinephrine (commonly called adrenaline), which is associated with feelings of alertness, fear, and anxiety. Another neurotransmitter that is thought to play a role in panic disorder is gamma-aminobutyric acid, or GABA. This is an inhibitor chemical because it helps balance excitation in the brain by preventing neurons from overfiring, as psychiatrist Carol W. Berman explains: "If the GABA system is not working well, nerve cells are not turned off (inhibited) when they should be and excess stimulation can occur, resulting in panic attacks and other unwanted events."[43]

Faulty Fight or Flight

Since the brain works in tandem with the nervous system, the latter is also believed to play a key role in the development of panic disorder. Scientists are especially curious about a component of the nervous system known as the autonomic nervous system, which controls involuntary bodily actions such as heartbeat, breathing, widening or narrowing of blood vessels, perspiration, and hormone secretion. The autonomic nervous system is composed of two sections, the sympathetic and parasympathetic nervous systems, and both have very specific functions.

> "Since the brain works in tandem with the nervous system, the latter is also believed to play a key role in the development of panic disorder."

When the brain senses any sort of threat or danger, the sympathetic nervous system fires off signals to the adrenal glands on the kidneys, which respond by secreting hormones such as adrenaline. This prepares the body for what is known as fight or flight, as Steven J. Seay, a psychologist from Palm Beach County, Florida, explains: "Think about a time you unexpectedly encountered a *physical threat* in your environment. Maybe you were peacefully gardening when you happened upon a snake. Maybe you were out for a stroll when an unfamiliar dog ran up to you with its teeth bared. . . . What are your options?"[44] Seay goes on to explain that those options include staying to confront the predator (fight) or running away (flight).

In the same way that the sympathetic nervous system prepares the body to face physical threats, it also kicks in when the brain perceives intangible threats, such as extreme stress or emotional trauma. Says Seay: "Most of the daily threats we face have shifted from the tangible to the intangible. . . . These threats can't necessarily walk up to you and bite off your arm, but they threaten our rather complex mental lives and endanger our physical and emotional well-being."[45]

> **A fact about brain chemistry that is well known to scientists is that the brain's pH must be at the correct level to ensure proper functioning.**

When the brain perceives that a threat or danger has passed, the parasympathetic nervous system goes to work. Its role is to act as a stabilizing force, restoring the body to a normal, calmer state by lowering the heart rate and blood pressure. For reasons that are not clear, the parasympathetic nervous system does not seem to function properly in people with panic disorder, meaning that their bodies remain in the overly excited state. Says Paul Li, who is a lecturer of cognitive science with the University of California–Berkeley: "If the parasympathetic nervous system is somehow unable to do its job, a person will remain fired up and may experience the heightened arousal characteristic of a panic attack."[46]

Acid Brain?

A fact about brain chemistry that is well known to scientists is that the brain's pH must be at the correct level to ensure proper functioning. The term *pH* refers to how acidic a particular substance is. It is measured on a scale of 0 to 14, with 0 indicating the highest concentration of acid and 14 being the most basic, or alkaline. Pure water, for instance, has a pH of 7, which means it is equally balanced between acid and alkaline. Applying this concept to the human body, research has shown that the brain's pH levels should be about 7.4. It is essential that the number not be much higher or lower than that, as University of California–Davis psychiatrist Richard Maddock explains: "In general, the pH of our brain is carefully regulated. A large increase or decrease in brain acidity can seriously disrupt brain functioning."[47]

Studies conducted by John Wemmie, who is an associate professor of psychiatry at the University of Iowa's Carver College of Medicine, have focused on the connection between pH levels in the brain and the development of conditions such as depression, anxiety, and panic disorder. In research with laboratory mice, Wemmie discovered that when pH is too low (meaning too acidic), it can lead to heightened anxiety and panic attacks. According to Maddock, such research shows "that brain pH changes are a crucial part of the mechanism of many fear behaviors."[48] Wemmie plans to continue his studies in an effort to further investigate the association between pH and panic disorder.

Uncertainty Lingers

Even though scientists have studied panic disorder for decades, they still do not know exactly what causes it. Research has yielded many promising findings, however, and this has led to theories about the contribution of genetics, brain chemistry, and environment, and how these factors might work together. As mysterious as panic disorder is, the key to discovering its cause lies in greater scientific understanding, which will undoubtedly continue to broaden in the coming years.

What Causes Panic Disorder?

66 **It's not known why a panic attack occurs when there's no obvious danger present.** 99

—Mayo Clinic, "Panic Attacks and Panic Disorder," May 31, 2012. www.mayoclinic.com.

The Mayo Clinic is a world-renowned medical facility headquartered in Rochester, Minnesota.

....

66 **A tendency to have panic attacks can be inherited. It's thought that first-degree biological relatives of individuals with panic disorder are eight times more likely to develop panic attacks.** 99

—Carol W. Berman, *100 Questions & Answers About Panic Disorder*. Sudbury, MA: Jones and Bartlett, 2010.

Berman is a clinical instructor of psychiatry at New York University Medical School.

....

* Editor's Note: While the definition of a primary source can be narrowly or broadly defined, for the purposes of Compact Research, a primary source consists of: 1) results of original research presented by an organization or researcher; 2) eyewitness accounts of events, personal experience, or work experience; 3) first-person editorials offering pundits' opinions; 4) government officials presenting political plans and/or policies; 5) representatives of organizations presenting testimony or policy.

Primary Source Quotes

> **According to one theory of panic disorder, the body's normal 'alarm system,' the set of mental and physical mechanisms that allows a person to respond to a threat, tends to be triggered unnecessarily, when there is no danger.**

—Roxanne Dryden-Edwards, "Panic Disorder," MedicineNet, March 24, 2011. www.medicinenet.com.

Dryden-Edwards is an adult, child, and adolescent psychiatrist.

> **Various imaging studies have found that the parts of the brain that control fear are different in people who suffer from panic attacks. In other words, some people are born with a higher risk of suffering panic attacks.**

—Anthony Komaroff, "What Is the Treatment for Panic Attacks?," Ask Doctor K., January 17, 2012. www.askdoctork.com.

Komaroff is a professor of medicine at Harvard Medical School.

> **It is common clinical experience that patients often present with panic disorder after a major loss, separation or illness of a significant other, or sexual or physical assault.**

—Dan J. Stein, Eric Hollander, and Barbara O. Rothbaum, *Textbook of Anxiety Disorders*. Arlington, VA: American Psychiatric, 2010.

Stein is a psychiatrist from Cape Town, South Africa; Hollander is a psychiatrist from New York City, and Rothbaum is a psychiatry professor at Atlanta's Emory University.

> **The cause of this condition is still not understood, but we have long known that the vulnerability to panic disorder is strongly genetic.**

—Richard Maddock, "Panic Attacks as a Problem of pH," *Scientific American*, May 18, 2010. www.scientificamerican.com.

Maddock is a professor of psychiatry at the University of California–Davis.

❝The causes of panic disorder involve a combination of heredity, chemical imbalances in the brain, and personal stress. Sudden losses or major life changes may trigger the onset of panic attacks.❞

—Edmund J. Bourne, *The Anxiety & Phobia Workbook*. Oakland, CA: New Harbinger, 2010.

Bourne is a psychologist who specializes in the treatment of anxiety, phobias, and other mental health disorders.

❝The risk of developing panic disorder is particularly high for female relatives of people with this disorder, whereas the male relatives of people with panic disorder are at particular risk for problems related to alcohol use.❞

—Lourie W. Reichenberg and Linda Seligman, *Selecting Effective Treatments: A Comprehensive, Systematic Guide to Treating Mental Disorders*. Hoboken, NJ: Wiley, 2012.

Reichenberg is a licensed professional counselor from Falls Church, Virginia, and Seligman (who died in 2007) was a professor emeritus of counseling and development at George Mason University.`

What Causes Panic Disorder?

- According to University of Maryland Medical Center, up to **50 percent** of people with panic disorder have close relatives who also suffer from the disorder, which suggests that heredity is a factor in who develops it.

- The Mayo Clinic states that people have a higher risk of developing panic disorder if their temperament is **highly susceptible to stress**.

- According to psychiatrist Carol W. Berman, immediate family members of panic disorder sufferers have **four to seven times** the risk of developing the disorder than that of the general population.

- An August 2010 paper by the Cleveland Clinic states that one theory about how anxiety disorders develop is disruptions in the **central nervous system**.

- According to psychiatrist Jack M. Gorman, someone's risk for panic disorder increases if he or she has suffered **severe emotional trauma during childhood**, such as parental death or divorce or sexual or physical abuse.

- A March 2011 paper by psychiatrist Mohammed A. Memon states that magnetic resonance imaging studies have found that patients with panic disorder have **smaller-than-average temporal lobe regions** of the brain.

A Complex Interaction

As with most mental illnesses, scientists do not know exactly what causes panic disorder. Based on years of research, most are convinced that multiple factors are involved, including genetics, brain chemistry, and environment.

Genetics
Up to 50 percent of panic disorder patients have family members who suffer from it

Brain Chemistry
Imbalance in chemical messengers known as neurotransmitters (serotonin, dopamine, GABA)

Environmental factors
Extreme stress, influence of family behavior (for example, a parent who suffers from panic attacks)

Panic Disorder

Brain structure
Part of the brain known as the fear center might not function properly

Life experience
Child abuse, traumatic events

Source: Harvey Simon, "Panic Disorder with Agoraphobia Overview," *New York Times*, February 8, 2012.

- According to psychiatrist Carol W. Berman, **lack of sleep** may stimulate certain hormones or other chemicals in the body to cause panic attacks.

- According to the Cleveland Clinic, a twenty-year study of the offspring of parents with depression found a **threefold increase** in anxiety disorders compared with the general population.

Females Have Highest Risk for Panic Disorder

Research has consistently shown that females are diagnosed with panic disorder at two to three times the rate of males. Scientists offer several theories to explain this, including hormonal fluctuations, a higher likelihood of childhood sexual abuse, and the fact that women are more likely to seek help for anxiety-related issues. A 2011 study by researchers from New York and Maryland found that of 929 people who suffered from panic disorder, nearly three-fourths were female.

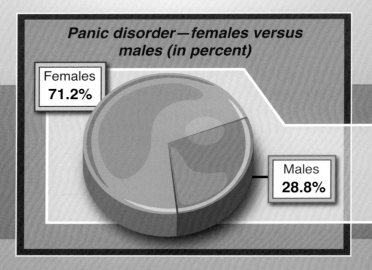

Panic disorder—females versus males (in percent)

Females
71.2%

Males
28.8%

Source: Jonathan S. Comer et al., "Health-Related Quality of Life Across the Anxiety Disorders," *Journal of Clinical Psychiatry*, January 2011. www.ncbi.nlm.nih.gov.

- The American Psychological Association states that the development of panic disorder has been associated with **major life transitions** that are particularly stressful, such as graduating from college, getting married, and having a first child.

- According to the Anxiety & Panic Disorder Center of Los Angeles, most patients with panic disorder grew up in homes where **emotions and expressing oneself were not encouraged**.

What Are the Effects of Panic Disorder?

❝People who have full-blown, repeated panic attacks can become very disabled by their condition.❞

—NIMH, the largest scientific organization in the world dedicated to research focused on mental disorders and the promotion of mental health.

❝There's emotional pain in panic. The fear, the sense of regret, the withering self-esteem . . . it hurts.❞

—Summer Beretsky, a young woman who struggled with panic disorder throughout college and graduate school.

Michael E. Brooks is a historian, college professor, and writer from Ohio who has battled panic disorder for much of his adult life. His panic attacks range in severity from fairly mild to so intensely frightening that he is almost paralyzed with fear. Brooks says that during the worst attacks, logical thought is crowded out by the irrational certainty that he is about to die. That is what happened one afternoon while he was alone in the kitchen and was suddenly terrified that an intruder was in the house and intended to kill him. He sat in a chair, not moving a muscle, staring at a closet door that was open just a crack. "I imagined that someone was watching me from behind this door," says Brooks. "This is when the panic attack kicked into overdrive, and for about 15 minutes I was in that near-paralytic state where every shadow movement (real or imagined in the normal afternoon lighting) was the first step in the last minutes of my life."[49]

Although Brooks only has a panic attack every two to three months, when an especially bad one strikes the fear is overpowering. He writes: "It is difficult to describe the confluence of dread, fright, and anger that result from the overdose of adrenaline in such a severe attack. . . . Again, logic falls by the wayside in this clenched-fists, gritted-teeth state."[50]

Diminished Joy

Many who live with panic disorder can relate to what Brooks has described because they face numerous struggles on a daily basis. The fear and dread that are characteristic of panic disorder can take a heavy toll on people's emotional and physical health and severely impair their quality of life. The disorder is associated with numerous problems, including a markedly higher risk of alcohol and drug abuse; dependence on others for financial help; a loss of interest in hobbies, sports, and other activities that were once enjoyable; and strained relationships with friends and family. One sufferer candidly expresses how tough it can be to live with panic disorder: "Dealing with this disorder is pure hell. . . . It's a very disabling and real condition that the general public doesn't understand. If I had a dime for every time I was told 'Why don't you just get over it, the attacks can't hurt you,' I'd be rich."[51]

> **The fear and dread that are characteristic of panic disorder can take a heavy toll on people's emotional and physical health and severely impair their quality of life.**

Throughout the years, several studies have focused on how anxiety disorders affect people's quality of life. For one that was published in January 2011, a team of researchers from New York and Maryland performed an in-depth analysis of national surveys of over forty-three thousand adults in the United States. The team found that nearly 10 percent of the people surveyed had one or more anxiety disorders, and of those, 2.2 percent suffered from panic disorder. Generalized anxiety disorder was found to have the most negative effect on quality of life and was closely followed by panic disorder. An especially startling finding of the study was that panic disorder resulted in poorer emotional well-being than serious illnesses such as cancer, diabetes, heart disease, and arthritis.

The Mental Illness Stigma

Society's overall perception of panic disorder poses difficult and painful challenges for people who suffer from this condition. It is not uncommon for them to face doubt and scorn from friends and acquaintances, be passed over for job promotions, encounter discrimination by potential employers, and even be dismissed by doctors who have little or no understanding of anxiety disorders. This can cause shame and embarrassment for sufferers, who then go out of their way to hide their illness. John Tsilimparis, a therapist with the Anxiety & Panic Disorder Center of Los Angeles, writes: "Panic disorder is not an easy thing to share with people because usually people react in a naïve manner by saying things like, 're- lax,' and 'don't worry so much.' Patients are then left feeling inadequate because they have no control over the symptoms others are insensitively trivializing. It is like telling a raging alcoholic not to drink or a Tourettes disorder sufferer not to tic."[52]

> " Sufferers know that they cannot prevent [panic] attacks, nor can they stop an attack once it starts, and they have no way of knowing where or when the next one might strike. "

A man named Marvin, who has battled panic disorder for years, often becomes frustrated over society's attitude toward those who suffer from the disorder. Because he knows how misinformed and unthinking people can be, he rarely discusses his illness. "The stigma part bothers me," he says. "I don't go around telling everyone that I have panic disorder and I'm proud of it." Marvin is convinced that it would be easier to be open with people if he had a physical disease like diabetes, rather than a mental illness. "As it is," he says, "to admit to panic is to say you're a wimp or chicken about something. I want to be seen as a strong man so women will be attracted to me and men will feel I'm reliable. Who wants to be seen as weak and frightened?" Marvin is convinced that famous and influential people can get away with freely admitting to having a mental illness, whereas the same is not true for the average person. "If another guy admits he has panic disorder," he says, "I might share that I have it too, but then again I might not. . . . The stigma is there, and it's not going away anytime soon."[53]

The Sheer Misery of Agoraphobia

For people with panic disorder, the never-ending fear and dread of having panic attacks can be crippling. Sufferers know that they cannot prevent the attacks, nor can they stop an attack once it starts, and they have no way of knowing where or when the next one might strike. This can lead to a growing fear of any situation or place from which they might be trapped and unable to escape. As this fear continues to deepen, many sufferers become convinced that there is only one place where they can be safe: their homes. The American Psychological Association writes: "In worst case scenarios, people with panic disorder develop agoraphobia . . . because they believe that by staying inside, they can avoid all situations that might provoke an attack, or where they might not be able to get help. The fear of an attack is so debilitating, they prefer to spend their lives locked inside their homes."[54]

> " Anxiety disorders are believed to have a strong association with suicide, but proving that has been challenging for researchers. "

In March 2010 a young man posted on a self-help website about his painful descent into agoraphobia. As is characteristic of those who have the disorder, he started by avoiding certain places that he feared would trigger a panic attack. This, he says, "was the first step to letting it fully control my life. It only took a few more attacks to make me terrified of having another, which often induced a panic attack in itself." The man started leaving work at odd times because he was so afraid of having a panic attack while he was there, and for the same reason, he stopped going other places, too: "I couldn't go into big grocery stores. I couldn't go to parties. Eventually I was freaking out so much at work, it was either I quit or they fire me."[55]

The man ended up quitting his job and moving back in with his parents. He hoped this would allow him to work on the anxiety that was at the root of his attacks, but he just continued to grow more reclusive. "Instead of using my parents' home as a place to get better," he says, "I got lazy and used it as an excuse to not face my fears. Eventually this led to me having full-blown agoraphobia so bad that I couldn't even walk to the end of the driveway to check the mail without severe anxiety."[56]

The Lingering Torment of War

An alarming number of military veterans, especially those who have served in war zones, suffer from severe psychological and emotional problems after they return home from active duty. According to a 2011 study by researchers from Charleston, South Carolina, one of the most serious of these problems is panic disorder. The research team conducted mental health evaluations of nearly nine hundred veterans who had sought medical care and found that over 8 percent had developed panic disorder, compared with an estimated 2.7 percent of the general population. Those who had the disorder suffered from a significant number of problems, including overall poor health, chronic pain, impaired emotional well-being, and social difficulties. Another finding of the study was that a high number of veterans suffered from both PTSD and panic disorder.

> **Life is far from easy for people with panic disorder.**

One female veteran who served as a specialist with the US Army is plagued by both disorders, and this has caused her immense emotional pain and turmoil. The woman was stationed in Iraq and began to have panic attacks eight months after returning home to Minnesota. The first attack struck while she was on a city bus because the loud rumbling noises brought back memories of riding in a Humvee. She had participated in numerous missions in which she rode in one of the canvas-sided military vehicles and performed her duties as a turret gunner, a job that she describes as "one of the most dangerous things you can do."[57] After the first panic attack, the woman began to have nightmares about the unspeakable horrors she saw in Iraq: her army buddies being wounded and killed and the many Iraqi civilians who were badly injured. Her panic attacks grew in severity until she became too frightened to leave her house, and this filled her with a deep sense of despair and hopelessness that continues to haunt her. "I feel worthless,"[58] she says.

Giving Up Hope

A tragic reality about mental illness is that it is associated with an extraordinarily high suicide risk. Studies have shown that about half the people who have suicidal thoughts and up to 90 percent of those who actually commit suicide suffer from some type of mental illness. Anxiety disorders are believed to have a strong association with suicide, but proving that has been challenging for researchers. Because a significant number of anxiety disorder sufferers have other related conditions, it is difficult to know whether a suicide resulted from the anxiety disorder, the other illness, or from the combination of them.

To investigate the possible connection between anxiety disorders and suicide, researchers from Canada's University of Manitoba conducted a study that was published in September 2010. It was based on data from national surveys of nearly thirty-five thousand American adults, of whom 3.4 percent had attempted suicide. Of those, over 70 percent were found to have suffered from at least one anxiety disorder. Based on comprehensive analysis, which included adjustments for other mental illnesses, the team determined that there was, in fact, a significant association between suicide and panic disorder.

Brittany is a panic disorder sufferer who attempted suicide when she was sixteen years old. That was a particularly rough time in her life, as she writes: "I had started skipping school more days than I attended because I was so overwhelmed. I found out that I was going to fail the year because of my absences. I remember thinking I couldn't tell my mom I was failing and believing that my life was pointless." Filled with despair and thoughts of no longer wanting to live, Brittany took an overdose of sleeping pills—and then immediately regretted what she had done. She reached out for help by calling 911 and in the process, saved her own life. "I was so ashamed," she says, "and I just knew something had to change."[59]

A Tough Way to Live

Life is far from easy for people with panic disorder. Along with suffering from terrifying panic attacks, they must cope with a society that is often intolerant of mental illness in any form, which can cause them to feel embarrassed and ashamed. For many, the fear of panic attacks becomes so consuming that they feel safe only when they are locked inside their homes—and some find the despair so unbearable that life no longer seems worth living.

What Are the Effects of Panic Disorder?

"Adolescents with panic disorder may self-medicate, leading to substance abuse."

—Jeffrey S. Forrest, "Pediatric Panic Disorder," Medscape, December 16, 2011. http://emedicine.medscape.com.

Forrest is a physician who contributes medical articles to the Medscape website.

"A person cannot die from panic attacks, although often people having panic attacks feel as though they might die."

—Carol W. Berman, *100 Questions & Answers About Panic Disorder*. Sudbury, MA: Jones and Bartlett, 2010.

Berman is a clinical instructor of psychiatry at New York University Medical School.

"Panic attacks in children may result in the child's grades declining, avoiding school and other separations from parents, as well as substance abuse, depression, and suicidal thoughts, plans, and/or actions."

—Roxanne Dryden-Edwards, "Panic Disorder," MedicineNet, March 24, 2011. www.medicinenet.com.

Dryden-Edwards is an adult, child, and adolescent psychiatrist.

* Editor's Note: While the definition of a primary source can be narrowly or broadly defined, for the purposes of Compact Research, a primary source consists of: 1) results of original research presented by an organization or researcher; 2) eyewitness accounts of events, personal experience, or work experience; 3) first-person editorials offering pundits' opinions; 4) government officials presenting political plans and/or policies; 5) representatives of organizations presenting testimony or policy.

❝A given person may have infrequent panic attacks, with little impact, or may have many attacks each week, resulting in considerable distress and impairment.❞

—Lourie W. Reichenberg and Linda Seligman, *Selecting Effective Treatments: A Comprehensive, Systematic Guide to Treating Mental Disorders*. Hoboken, NJ: Wiley, 2012.

Reichenberg is a licensed professional counselor from Falls Church, Virginia, and Seligman (who died in 2007) was a professor emeritus of counseling and development at George Mason University.

❝Left untreated, panic attacks and panic disorder can result in severe complications that affect almost every area of your life.❞

—Mayo Clinic, "Panic Attacks and Panic Disorder," May 31, 2012. www.mayoclinic.com.

The Mayo Clinic is a world-renowned medical facility headquartered in Rochester, Minnesota.

❝Persons with agoraphobia may become homebound because they fear they may have a panic attack when they are out of their comfort zone.❞

—Janet M. Torpy, "Panic Disorder," *Journal of the American Medical Association*, March 23, 2011. http://jama.jamanetwork.com.

Torpy is a physician who often writes on behalf of the American Medical Association.

❝The risk of coronary artery disease in patients with panic disorder is nearly doubled.❞

—Mohammed A. Memon, "Panic Disorder," Medscape, March 29, 2011. http://emedicine.medscape.com/article/287913-overview#aw2aab6b2b4aa.

Memon is chair of the Department of Psychiatry at the Spartanburg Regional Medical Center in Spartanburg, South Carolina.

66 **Panic disorder is frightening because of the panic attacks associated with it, and also because it often leads to other complications such as phobias, depression, substance abuse, medical complications, even suicide.** 99

—American Psychological Association, "Answers to Your Questions About Panic Disorder," 2012. www.apa.org.

The American Psychological Association is a scientific and professional organization that represents the field of psychology in the United States.

66 **Panic disorder often coexists with unexplained medical problems, such as chest pain not associated with a heart attack or chronic fatigue.** 99

—Mental Health America, "Panic Disorder," 2012. www.mentalhealthamerica.net.

Mental Health America is dedicated to helping all people live mentally healthier lives and educating the public about mental health and mental illness.

What Are the Effects of Panic Disorder?

- According to psychiatrist Mohammed A. Memon, substance abuse among people with panic disorder is up to **fourteen times higher** than that of the general population.

- The National Institutes of Health states that people with panic disorder are more likely to be **unemployed, be less productive at work, and have difficult personal relationships**, including marital problems.

- A study published in September 2010 by researchers from Manitoba, Canada, found that among individuals reporting a lifetime history of attempted suicide, over **70 percent** had an anxiety disorder.

- According to psychiatrist Jack M. Gorman, if someone's panic disorder is not identified after the first attack, the condition can become **extremely debilitating**.

- The American Psychological Association states that the most immediate danger of panic disorder is that it can lead to **phobias**.

- According to the South African Depression and Anxiety Group, up to **30 percent** of people with panic disorder abuse alcohol, **17 percent** abuse drugs, and up to **20 percent** attempt suicide.

- A 2011 paper by Columbia University researcher Renee D. Goodwin and colleagues states that over **37 percent** of adults with panic disorder have lifetime alcohol abuse or dependence.

Panic Disorder Impairs Quality of Life

People with panic disorder often struggle with emotional problems and other issues that can have a detrimental effect on their quality of life.

Panic disorder sufferers . . .

are more prone to alcohol and drug abuse

have greater risk of suicidal thoughts and attempts

spend more time in hospital emergency rooms

spend less time on hobbies, sports, and other enjoyable activities

tend to be financially dependent on others

feel emotionally and physically less healthy than nonsufferers

are afraid of driving more than a few miles from home

are at higher risk of losing their jobs and having to rely on public assistance or family members

Source: American Psychological Association, "Answers to Your Questions About Panic Disorder," 2012. www.apa.org.

- Massachusetts General Hospital states that children with panic disorder may develop **depression** or even have thoughts of **not wanting to be alive** because they mistakenly believe that no one can help them.

- According to clinical counselor Sheryl Ankrom, people with panic disorder are up to seven times more likely to suffer from **migraine headaches**.

- Psychiatrist Mohammed A. Memon states that lifetime rates of major depression range from **50 to 60 percent** in people with panic disorder.

Panic Disorder and Poor Health

Research has shown that people with panic disorder often develop serious health problems such as heart conditions. This was confirmed in a study published in 2011 by researchers from New York and Maryland, who found that panic disorder sufferers are affected by a number of medical issues at a rate that is much higher than those who do not have the disorder.

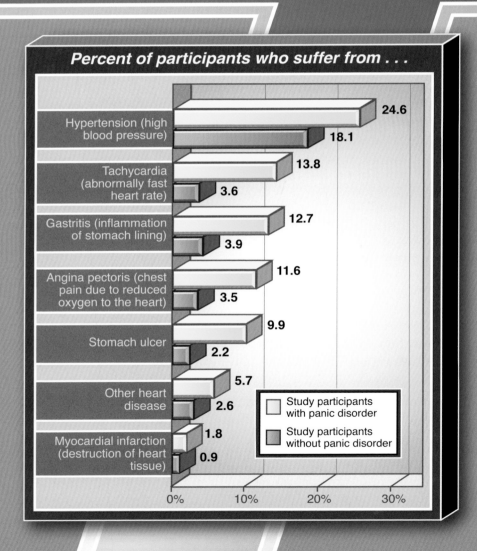

Percent of participants who suffer from . . .

Condition	With panic disorder	Without panic disorder
Hypertension (high blood pressure)	24.6	18.1
Tachycardia (abnormally fast heart rate)	13.8	3.6
Gastritis (inflammation of stomach lining)	12.7	3.9
Angina pectoris (chest pain due to reduced oxygen to the heart)	11.6	3.5
Stomach ulcer	9.9	2.2
Other heart disease	5.7	2.6
Myocardial infarction (destruction of heart tissue)	1.8	0.9

Study participants with panic disorder
Study participants without panic disorder

Source: Jonathan S. Comer et al., "Health-Related Quality of Life Across the Anxiety Disorders," *Journal of Clinical Psychiatry*, January 2011. www.ncbi.nlm.nih.gov.

Familial Risk of Alcohol Abuse

For a study published in 2011 a team of researchers from the United States and Israel examined the connection between panic disorder and alcohol abuse. They found that immediate family members (such as a parent or sibling) of people with panic disorder have a significant risk of developing alcohol problems, with the greatest risk among relatives of people with both panic disorder and alcohol abuse.

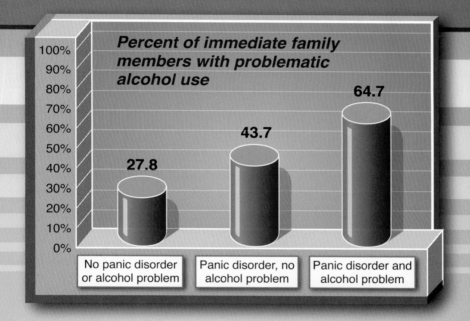

Percent of immediate family members with problematic alcohol use

	No panic disorder or alcohol problem	Panic disorder, no alcohol problem	Panic disorder and alcohol problem
	27.8	43.7	64.7

Source: Renee D. Goodwin et al., "Family History of Alcohol Use Disorders Among Adult with Panic Disorder in the Community," *Journal of Psychiatric Research*, August 2011. https://katherinekeyes.wikischolars.columbia.edu.

- According to researchers from the United Kingdom, people with panic disorder have a higher risk of developing **heart disease or suffering a heart attack** than do those in the general population, with the greatest risk among younger people.

Can People Overcome Panic Disorder?

66Panic disorder is one of the most treatable of all the anxiety disorders, responding in most cases to certain kinds of medication or certain kinds of cognitive psychotherapy, which help change thinking patterns that lead to fear and anxiety.99

—NIMH, the largest scientific organization in the world dedicated to research focused on mental disorders and the promotion of mental health.

66Sadly, many people with panic attacks do not seek or receive treatment.99

—Roxanne Dryden-Edwards, an adult, child, and adolescent psychiatrist.

In November 2011 the online magazine *YC Teen* published a story written by a teenage girl who was able to overcome panic disorder. The girl explained how she had experienced panic attacks on and off throughout her life, but one that struck after a terrifying nightmare was worse than anything she could have imagined—and caused her to fear that she was losing her mind. After the attack she huddled in her room, alone and afraid. "It felt like the old me had rotted away," she says, "and left only weak, shaken bones behind. I wanted to go back to normal."[60] The fear lingered for days, until the girl could not take it any longer and reached out for help. Finally having the courage to do so was a relief for her, but it also spawned a new fear that she might end up in a mental institution for life. On the way to her appointment for a psychiatric evaluation, she was filled with a sense of dread, as she explains: "I thought they would find out that I was some soon-to-be-crazy person and lock me up."[61]

She soon learned how wrong she was. The doctor was very familiar with anxiety disorders, and after an extensive evaluation, she knew that the girl was suffering from panic disorder and referred her to a therapist. Through therapy the girl identified her fears, learned how to work through them, and began the process of healing. At the time she wrote her story, she had been panic free for over a year and had rediscovered the joy of life. "Sometimes I get scared that I might have another panic attack," she says, "but I remember my therapist's quote: 'Whatever it is, I shall overcome it.'"[62]

Tried and True Therapy

The girl's fear that she was losing her mind may have been irrational, but this sort of worry is not uncommon among people with panic disorder. Their panic attacks are so terrifying that they cannot imagine any sane person feeling the way they do. For that reason, along with shame and embarrassment, most panic disorder sufferers never seek treatment. This is unfortunate, because the disorder is one of the most treatable of all mental illnesses, as psychiatrist Carol W. Berman explains: "Each new patient has a 90% chance to be panic attack–free in a month or sooner with the right treatment. Not all people suffering from mental disorders are as fortunate as panic attack patients, who usually have such a good prognosis."[63]

Mental health professionals widely agree that therapy is an essential part of panic disorder treatment, and one type that has proved to be especially effective is CBT. It is based on the premise that sufferers are more frightened of their fears than of certain situations or events, as

> **Mental health professionals widely agree that therapy is an essential part of panic disorder treatment, and one type that has proved to be especially effective is CBT.**

psychologist Ben Martin explains: "CBT is based on a model or theory that it's not events themselves that upset us, but the meanings we give them. If our thoughts are too negative, it can block us seeing things or doing things that don't fit—that disconfirm—what we believe is true. In other words, we continue to hold on to the same old thoughts and fail to learn anything new."[64] CBT differs from other psychotherapies because sessions are structured and focused on particular problems and goals, whereas some types of therapy involve patients talking freely to a therapist about whatever comes to mind.

According to Berman, a technique known as conditioning is a valuable part of CBT. It was designed around the idea that over time, patients have become conditioned to think in negative ways. Thus, they must be reconditioned to replace this negativity with more positive thinking. Berman writes: "Conditioning is the process of acquiring, developing, educating, establishing, learning, or training new responses in an individual. When the triggers of a panic attack are identified, those events that cause an automatic response, behavioral therapy can help unlink those triggers."[65]

Berman uses the example of a woman who always has panic attacks whenever she rides a bus. Through conditioning she learns how to replace muscle tenseness, shallow breathing, and fear images with muscle relaxation, deep breathing, and peaceful images, and she can use these tools to help avoid a panic attack (or lessen the severity of one) the next time she is on a bus. Says Berman: "Panic attack patients can be taught to disregard many of the bodily sensations of which they are hyperaware, for example, heart palpitations and tingling in the arms and legs. Instead of concentrating on these meaningless feelings, they learn how to breathe deeply and to imagine pleasant things if a panic attack begins."[66]

Deliberate Fear Exposure

A form of CBT known as interoceptive exposure (or exposure therapy) works well for many people with panic disorder. This technique requires sufferers to face their fears head-on as an approach to overcoming them. Although this can be terrifying for patients, confronting fear can help them break unhealthy habits such as the instinctive need to avoid objects or situations that evoke fear. The American Psychological Association explains: "Interoceptive exposure can help them go through the symptoms of an attack (elevated heart rate, hot flashes, sweating, and so on) in a controlled setting, and teach them that these symptoms need not develop into a full-blown attack." The American Psychological Association adds that a technique known as in vivo exposure can be a valuable part of exposure therapy. This involves "breaking a fearful situation down into small manageable steps and doing them one at a time until the most difficult level is mastered."[67]

Many psychologists believe that exposure therapy is one of the most effective treatments for panic disorder because it zeroes in on the fear of having panic attacks, which is one of the worst problems for sufferers. Specifically, sufferers become hypersensitive to bodily sensations such as increased heart rate, difficulty breathing, dizziness, and feelings of unreality, as all these are symptomatic of an impending panic attack. Through exposure therapy, the person engages in exercises that are intended to trigger these sensations, and the exercises are repeated until the person becomes desensitized (or used to) the sensations.

> " Although this can be terrifying for patients, confronting fear can help them break unhealthy habits such as the instinctive need to avoid objects or situations that evoke fear. "

Some of these exercises include breathing through a straw or breathing rapidly, which can induce a racing heart, shortness of breath, and dizziness; and spinning around in a circle or shaking one's head from side to side to induce dizziness and lightheadedness. Says psychologist Charles H. Elliott: "There are various additional techniques for creating similar sensations. By repeating these exercises over and over again, you gradually learn that you won't go crazy; you're not going to die, and most importantly, that you can cope with anxious feelings. That knowledge allows you to quit worrying about having panic attacks which usually helps them fade from the scene."[68]

The Pros and Cons of Medications

Although mental health professionals widely agree that therapy is an essential part of panic disorder treatment, many are convinced that the most effective treatment is a combination of therapy and medication. Says the

Mars, Pennsylvania, psychological group Malec, Herring, and Krause: "Antidepressant and antianxiety medications can help restore the balance of biochemicals in the brain associated with anxiety disorders. This often helps a person benefit more quickly from the other elements of their treatment."[69] Depending on the patient's individual needs, different types of medications may be prescribed, with one of the most common being antidepressants. In the past these drugs were only prescribed for patients with depression, but because they alter brain chemistry, they have proved to be effective for treating panic disorder as well. Selective serotonin reuptake inhibitors, for instance, can help restore serotonin levels in the brain to normal, so they are often recommended for panic disorder patients.

As popular as medications are for treating panic disorder, not all mental health professionals have a favorable opinion of them. Many believe that the medications only mask panic attack symptoms and do nothing to get at the root of a patient's problems, which can only occur through therapy. Martin shares his thoughts: "CBT can substantially reduce the symptoms of many emotional disorders—clinical trials have shown this. In the short term, it's just as good as drug therapies at treating depression and anxiety disorders. And the benefits may last longer. All too often, when drug treatments finish, people relapse, and so practitioners may advise patients to continue using medication for longer."[70]

> "As popular as medications are for treating panic disorder, not all mental health professionals have a favorable opinion of them."

Despite objections such as these, many panic disorder patients are convinced that medications have made a major difference in their recovery. Brittany, whose treatment has included both therapy and antianxiety medication, credits this combination with her ability to overcome panic disorder. She says that the medication does not take away her anxiety, but brings it down to a level where she can cope, and she now has very few panic attacks. She writes: "I've gone through phases in my life when I have taken myself off the medication. But . . . it doesn't take long for me to start feeling like my life is too much for me to handle. I have accepted that I will be on medication for the rest of my life."[71]

Treatment in a Ring

For years scientists have known about the value of biofeedback for treating numerous diseases and disorders. Biofeedback is a technique in which patients tap into the power of the mind to control bodily functions such as heart rate, temperature, and blood pressure. Patients are connected to electrical sensors that help measure and receive information (feedback) about their bodies. The sensors eventually train them how to make subtle changes in order to achieve the desired results, such as reducing anxiety or pain. Says the Mayo Clinic: "In essence, biofeedback gives you the power to use your thoughts to control your body, often to help with a health condition or physical performance. Biofeedback is often used as a relaxation technique."[72]

In 2010 a team of researchers from Taiwan announced the development of a system that combines biofeedback with web technology, which allows panic disorder patients and medical providers to communicate online while engaging in therapy sessions. Patients wear a wireless-enabled finger ring that is designed to measure skin temperature. As they interact online with the therapist, the ring continuously monitors and records fluctuations in their body temperature, and this provides instant feedback to the therapist about how they are responding emotionally. Based on this feedback, patients learn how to reduce anxiety through relaxation techniques, as well as how to observe the effects of these techniques on skin temperature. According to Jerry Kennard, a psychologist from the United Kingdom, such tools "can reveal the amount of personal control we have over our responses and this provides a powerful method to control anxiety."[73]

> " Although panic disorder can be devastating for those who suffer from it, recovery is within reach with the appropriate treatment program. "

"No Reason to Suffer"

Although panic disorder can be devastating for those who suffer from it, recovery is within reach with the appropriate treatment program. Numerous options are available, including various types of therapy, medications, and alternative techniques such as biofeedback. All these have proved to be valuable in treating panic disorder, but overcoming it is only possible if people are willing to ask for help—and unfortunately most never do. Brittany is one person who did seek help, and she encourages others to do the same. "There is no reason to suffer in silence," she says. "This only makes it harder. Help could mean therapy, medication, or confiding in a loved one. Find something that works for you." Brittany also has words of advice for those who are struggling with panic disorder: "Don't stop living your life. There have been many times I didn't do something because I was scared, and I have regretted it. But the times I have soldiered on, have been the best and most rewarding experiences."[74]

Can People Overcome Panic Disorder?

❝Although your physician and the media may lead you to believe that medication is the best answer, it is not.❞

—Jennifer L. Abel, "Working Past Panic Attacks," January 4, 2011. www.anxietystlouispsychologist.com.

Abel is a clinical psychologist from Clayton, Missouri.

❝Somehow medications have acquired a bad reputation and patients believe they should try everything they can to stay away from medicine.❞

—Carol W. Berman, *100 Questions & Answers About Panic Disorder*. Sudbury, MA: Jones and Bartlett, 2010.

Berman is a clinical instructor of psychiatry at New York University Medical School.

❝Early treatment can help keep the disease from getting worse, and people can learn effective ways to live with [panic] disorder.❞

—Office on Women's Health, "Panic Disorder," March 29, 2010. http://womenshealth.gov.

An agency of the US Department of Health and Human Services, the Office on Women's Health is dedicated to helping women and girls be healthier and have a better sense of well-being.

* Editor's Note: While the definition of a primary source can be narrowly or broadly defined, for the purposes of Compact Research, a primary source consists of: 1) results of original research presented by an organization or researcher; 2) eyewitness accounts of events, personal experience, or work experience; 3) first-person editorials offering pundits' opinions; 4) government officials presenting political plans and/or policies; 5) representatives of organizations presenting testimony or policy.

66 **Although there are several effective treatments available for people with panic disorder, current treatments do not work for all patients.** 99

—Richard Maddock, "Panic Attacks as a Problem of pH," *Scientific American*, May 18, 2010. www.scientificamerican.com.

Maddock is a professor of psychiatry at the University of California–Davis.

66 **Most patients show significant progress after a few weeks of therapy. Relapses may occur, but they can often be effectively treated just like the initial episode.** 99

—Mental Health America, "Panic Disorder," 2012. www.mentalhealthamerica.net.

Mental Health America is dedicated to helping all people live mentally healthier lives and educating the public about mental health and mental illness.

66 **The first part of therapy is largely informational; many people are greatly helped by simply understanding exactly what panic disorder is, and how many others suffer from it.** 99

—American Psychological Association, "Answers to Your Questions About Panic Disorder," 2012. www.apa.org.

The American Psychological Association is a scientific and professional organization that represents the field of psychology in the United States.

66 **A range of drugs is now widely accepted to be effective in panic disorder.** 99

—Dan J. Stein, Eric Hollander, and Barbara O. Rothbaum, *Textbook of Anxiety Disorders*. Arlington, VA: American Psychiatric, 2010.

Stein is a psychiatrist from Cape Town, South Africa; Hollander is a psychiatrist from New York City; and Rothbaum is a psychiatry professor at Atlanta's Emory University.

66 Cognitive therapy in combination with some form of behavioral therapy has become the treatment of choice for panic disorder. **99**

—Lourie W. Reichenberg and Linda Seligman, *Selecting Effective Treatments: A Comprehensive, Systematic Guide to Treating Mental Disorders.* Hoboken, NJ: Wiley, 2012.

Reichenberg is a licensed professional counselor from Falls Church, Virginia, and Seligman (who died in 2007) was a professor emeritus of counseling and development at George Mason University.

Can People Overcome Panic Disorder?

- The South African Depression and Anxiety Group states that two-thirds of South Africans who suffer from panic disorder will **never seek help** due to the stigma of the illness.

- According to the Cleveland Clinic, patients who are treated with a combination of **CBT and medications** have twice the remission rate of other types of treatment.

- The National Institutes of Health states that developing a **dependence on medications** is a potential complication of panic disorder treatment.

- According to psychiatrist Mohammed A. Memon, nearly **65 percent** of patients who are treated for panic disorder achieve remission, typically within six months.

- In a 2010 publication, the NIMH states that medications called **beta blockers** can help control panic disorder symptoms such as excessive sweating, pounding heart, and dizziness.

- According to the American Psychiatric Association, **CBT** is the most effective type of therapy for treating panic disorder.

- According to psychiatrist Carol W. Berman, **antidepressants** have proved to be the best medications to control panic attacks.

Patients Say Combination Treatment Works Best

In July 2010, *Consumer Reports* published a survey of 1,544 readers who had sought help for anxiety disorders, depression, or both. As this graph shows, respondents who were treated with a combination of medicine and at least seven therapy sessions experienced the best results.

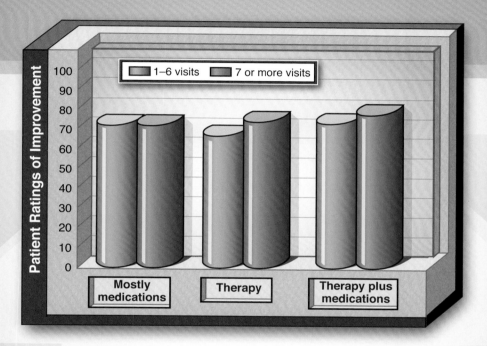

Source: *Consumer Reports*, "A Good Investment," July 2010. www.consumerreports.org.

- The US Food and Drug Administration has **not approved specific medications** for the treatment of panic disorder in children and adolescents.

- According to the Cleveland Clinic, antidepressants known as **selective serotonin reuptake inhibitors** have proved to be the most effective and best-tolerated medications for patients with panic disorder.

Therapy Helps Youth Overcome Panic Disorder

Mental health professionals stress that young people who suffer from panic disorder can benefit from counseling, which helps them understand that they suffer from a real illness rather than a bad attitude or flawed personality. Also, counseling can help reduce the impact of panic disorder symptoms. This table shows several types of counseling and the focus of each.

Individual psychotherapy

Generally recommended as the first line of treatment for children and adolescents with panic disorder. Can help reduce symptoms and help young people become aware of and address their feelings of failure and self-blame.

Cognitive behavioral therapy (CBT)

Teaches new skills to reduce anxiety that can lead to panic attacks. Patients learn to identify negative thoughts and use techniques for anticipating and preventing the emergence of full-blown panic attacks.

Parental guidance and family therapy

Can help parents to manage their child's illness, identify effective parenting skills, learn how to function as a family despite the illness, and to address complex feelings that can arise when raising a child with a psychiatric disorder.

Group psychotherapy

Provides a safe place to talk with other young people who face adversity and to practice social skills or symptom-combating skills in a structured setting.

School-based counseling

Helps young people with panic disorder navigate the social, behavioral, and academic demands of the school setting.

Source: Massachusetts General Hospital School Psychiatry Program & Madi Resource Center, "Panic Disorder," 2010. www.2massgeneral.org.

Hindrances to Treatment Progress

Research shows that people with panic disorder can benefit from treatment, and cognitive behavioral therapy (CBT) has proved to be especially effective. But in order for this technique to work, patients must be motivated, have positive expectations, and form a good relationship with the therapist, which is not always the case. This graph shows how a group of CBT therapists responded when asked about the patient factors that limit CBT's effectiveness in treating panic disorder.

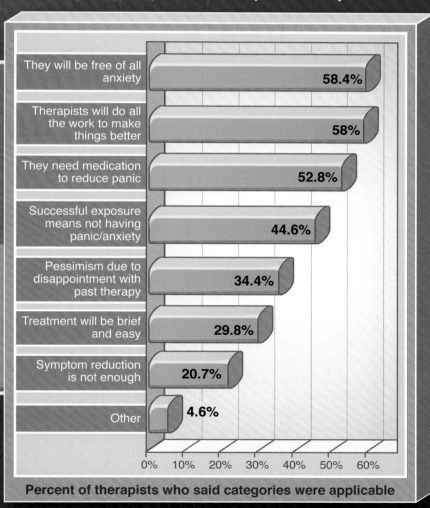

Therapist perspectives on patient expectations

- They will be free of all anxiety — **58.4%**
- Therapists will do all the work to make things better — **58%**
- They need medication to reduce panic — **52.8%**
- Successful exposure means not having panic/anxiety — **44.6%**
- Pessimism due to disappointment with past therapy — **34.4%**
- Treatment will be brief and easy — **29.8%**
- Symptom reduction is not enough — **20.7%**
- Other — **4.6%**

Percent of therapists who said categories were applicable

Source: American Psychological Association, Society of Clinical Psychology, "Clinicians' Experiences in Using an Empirically Supported Treatment (EST) for Panic Disorder: Results of a Survey," October 2010. www.div12.org.

Key People and Advocacy Groups

Anxiety Disorders Association of America: An advocacy group that is dedicated to the prevention, treatment, and cure of anxiety disorders.

Aaron Tempkin Beck: An American psychiatrist who is known as the father of CBT.

David D. Burns: A psychiatrist whose 1980 book *Feeling Good* raised awareness of the benefits of CBT for treating a number of mental illnesses, including panic disorder.

Albert Ellis: An American psychologist who developed one of the first forms of CBT (called rational emotive therapy) in the mid-1950s.

Sigmund Freud: An Austrian neurologist who wrote extensively about "anxiety neurosis" and panic and was the first to explore the connection between panic disorder and agoraphobia.

Donald F. Klein: A professor of psychiatry at Columbia University Medical Center and a leading panic disorder researcher who is credited with coining the term *panic attack*.

Henry Maudsley: A British psychiatrist who introduced the word *panic* into psychiatry when he described panic attacks in his 1879 book *The Pathology of Mind*.

National Anxiety Foundation: An organization whose goal is to educate the public about anxiety disorders.

National Institute of Mental Health: The largest scientific organization in the world dedicated to research focused on mental disorders and the promotion of mental health.

Carl Friedrich Otto Westphal: A German neurologist who was the first to use the term *agoraphobia* to describe patients who suffer from extreme dread when entering streets or public places.

Chronology

1752
French scientist François Boissier de Sauvages publishes a medical textbook in which he describes states of anxiety that involve intense shaking of the body and feelings of terror; he refers to this condition as "panophobia."

1952
The first edition of the American Psychiatric Association's *Diagnostic and Statistical Manual of Mental Disorders* is published, ushering in the formal classification of mental illnesses.

1895
Austrian neurologist Sigmund Freud publishes a paper in which he discusses his theories about anxiety neurosis and describes the spontaneous nature of panic attacks.

1750   **1850**   **1900**   **1950**

1871
German neurologist Carl Friedrich Otto Westphal introduces the term *agoraphobia* in describing three male patients who suffer from extreme dread when entering streets or public places.

1921
In experiments with frogs, Austrian scientist Otto Loewi discovers the neurotransmitter acetylcholine and correctly identifies its role in brain function.

1964
Columbia University psychiatrist Donald F. Klein publishes a study in which the antidepressant imipramine was found to be effective for patients suffering from panic attacks.

1879
In his book *The Pathology of Mind*, British psychiatrist Henry Maudsley introduces the word *panic* into psychiatry when he describes panic attacks.

1980
The American Psychiatric Association officially recognizes panic disorder as a mental illness when it is included in the third edition of the *Diagnostic and Statistical Manual of Mental Disorders*.

1991
The National Institutes of Health issues a statement saying that panic disorder affects at least one out of every seventy-five people worldwide.

2001
After studying families with a history of panic disorder, a team of researchers from Barcelona, Spain, discovers chromosomal abnormalities in 90 percent of affected family members, which suggests a genetic basis for the disorder.

1993
Columbia University psychiatrist Donald F. Klein reports that panic disorder is purely biological, meaning that it is caused by faulty brain wiring rather than environmental factors.

2010
University of Iowa researchers find that recurring panic attacks may be caused by imbalances of pH (acidity) at key junctures in the brain.

1990　　　　**2000**　　　　**2010**

1999
A study by researchers from Detroit's Henry Ford Health System finds a close connection between daily smoking and the development of panic disorder.

2003
In experiments with mice, researchers from Case Western Reserve University in Cleveland, Ohio, discover a gene that regulates levels of a chemical responsible for controlling anxiety, impulsive violence, and depression in humans.

2011
Researchers from Southern Methodist University in Dallas, Texas, publish a study showing that panic attacks are foreshadowed by subtle physical signals that begin at least sixty minutes before an attack.

1992
A study by researchers from Henry Ford Hospital in Detroit, Michigan, finds that young adults who suffer from migraine headaches are twelve times more likely to develop panic disorder than those with no history of migraine.

2012
University of Iowa psychiatry professor John Wemmie develops a new imaging technique that measures pH changes in the brain, which could provide clues about the relationship between brain acidity and panic disorder.

Related Organizations

American Psychological Association (APA)

50 First St. NE
Washington, DC 20002-4242
phone: (202) 336-5500; toll-free: (800) 374-2721
website: www.apa.org

The APA is a scientific and professional organization that represents the field of psychology in the United States. Its website links to newspaper articles, research data, and a number of online publications. It features a search engine that produces articles about panic attacks and panic disorder.

Anxiety and Depression Association of America (ADAA)

8730 Georgia Ave.
Silver Spring, MD 20910
phone: (240) 485-1001 • fax: (240) 485-1035
website: www.adaa.org

The ADAA seeks to prevent, treat, and cure anxiety disorders and depression while improving the lives of people who suffer from them. Its website features separate sections with information about the various anxiety disorders, including panic disorder and agoraphobia.

Anxiety Disorders Foundation

PO Box 560
Oconomowoc, WI 53066
phone: (262) 567-6600 • fax: (262) 567-7600
e-mail: info@anxietydisordersfoundation.org
website: www.anxietydisordersfoundation.org

The Anxiety Disorders Foundation is dedicated to improving the lives of everyone who is affected by anxiety disorders. It website has a special section that provides detailed information about the various anxiety disorders, including panic disorder.

Freedom from Fear

308 Seaview Ave.
Staten Island, NY 10305
phone: (718) 351-1717 • fax: (718) 980-5022
e-mail: help@freedomfromfear.org • website: www.freedomfromfear.org

Through advocacy, education, research, and community support, Freedom from Fear seeks to have a positive effect on the lives of people who suffer from anxiety, depression, and related disorders. Its website features an e-newsletter and detailed information about panic disorder and other anxiety disorders, including treatment options.

Mayo Clinic

200 First St. SW
Rochester, MN 55905
phone: (507) 284-2511 • fax: (507) 284-0161
website: www.mayoclinic.com

The Mayo Clinic is a world-renowned medical facility that is dedicated to patient care, education, and research. Its website offers separate sections on anxiety disorders and panic disorder, and both contain a great deal of information about causes, complications, treatment, and recovery.

Mental Health America

2000 N. Beauregard St., 6th Floor
Alexandria, VA 22311
phone: (703) 684-7722; toll-free: (800) 969-6642 • fax: (703) 684-5968
website: www.nmha.org

Mental Health America is dedicated to helping people live mentally healthier lives and educating the public about mental health and mental illness. The website's search engine produces a number of articles that discuss what panic disorder is, what causes it, challenges faced by people who suffer from it, and how it is treated.

National Alliance on Mental Illness (NAMI)

3803 N. Fairfax Dr., Suite 100
Arlington, VA 22203
phone: (703) 524-7600; toll-free: (800) 950-6264 • fax: (703) 524-9094
website: www.nami.org

The NAMI is dedicated to improving the lives of people who suffer from mental illness, as well as the lives of their families. Its website features fact sheets, news releases, online discussion groups, and a search engine that produces articles about panic disorder.

National Anxiety Foundation

3135 Custer Dr.
Lexington, KY 40517-4001
phone: (859) 272-7166
website: www.lexington-on-line.com/naf.html

The National Anxiety Foundation's goal is to educate the public about anxiety disorders. Its website features information about the various types of anxiety disorders, causes, treatment options, and suggestions for further research.

National Institute of Mental Health (NIMH)

Science Writing, Press, and Dissemination Branch
6001 Executive Blvd., Room 8184, MSC 9663
Bethesda, MD 20892-9663
phone: (301) 443-4513; toll-free: (866) 615-6464 • fax: (301) 443-4279
e-mail: nimhinfo@nih.gov • website: www.nimh.nih.gov

An agency of the National Institutes of Health, the NIMH is the largest scientific organization in the world dedicated to research on mental disorders and the promotion of mental health. Its website features statistics, archived *Science News* articles, and a search engine that produces numerous publications about anxiety disorders, including panic disorder.

University of California–Los Angeles Anxiety Disorders Research Center

Department of Psychology
Franz Hall—Box 951563
Los Angeles, CA 90094-1563
phone: (310) 206-9191 • fax: (310) 825-9048
e-mail: adrc@psych.ucla.edu • website: http://anxiety.psych.ucla.edu

The Anxiety Disorders Research Center seeks further understanding of the factors that place people at risk for developing anxiety disorders and to develop more effective treatments. Its website provides descriptions of panic disorder and other anxiety disorders, as well as information about current studies and treatment methods.

For Further Research

Books

Carol W. Berman, *100 Questions & Answers About Panic Disorder*. Sudbury, MA: Jones and Bartlett, 2010.

Edmund J. Bourne, *The Anxiety and Phobia Workbook*. Oakland, CA: New Harbinger, 2010.

Daniel Freeman and Jason Freeman, *Anxiety: A Very Short Introduction*. Oxford: Oxford University Press, 2012.

Anne Spencer, *I Get Panic Attacks: Now What?* New York: Rosen, 2012.

Robert E. Sterling, *I Made It Through the Rain: A Story About Overcoming Panic Disorder*. Bloomington, IN: iUniverse, 2011.

Priscilla Warner, *Learning to Breathe: My Yearlong Quest to Bring Calm to My Life*. New York: Free Press, 2011.

Periodicals

Sue Adair, "My Life Was Ruled by Fear," *Good Health*, April 1, 2011.

Nicole Elphick, "When Anxiety Attacks," *Cleo*, February 1, 2011.

Michael J. Formica, "Sleight of Gland: When Hormones Wreak Havoc," *Psychology Today*, November/December 2010.

Glamour, "Speaking Up About Anxiety," November 2010.

Good Health, "The Age of Anxiety," July 1, 2011.

Jan Goodwin, "The VA Health-Care System's Dishonorable Conduct," *Good Housekeeping*, March 2010.

Darrell Hulisz, "Treatment of Panic Disorder," *Chain Drug Review*, September 26, 2011.

USA Today (magazine), "Teenagers: Increased Stress Puts More at Risk," April 2012.

Hans Villarica, "The Upside of a Panic Attack: The Worst Is Over Before You Know It," *Atlantic*, September 2011.

Liz Welch, "Get Happier Guide," *Self*, May 2010.

Internet Sources

American Psychological Association, "Answers to Your Questions About Panic Disorder," 2012. www.apa.org/topics/anxiety/panic-disorder. aspx.

Anxiety in Teens – http://anxietyinteens.org. An online resource created for young people who suffer from anxiety disorders and other mental illnesses.

Sara Benincasa, "I Have Panic Attacks," *News* (blog), Frisky, April 14, 2010. www.thefrisky.com/2010-04-14/i-have-panic-attacks.

CNN, "Agoraphobia," April 21, 2011. www.cnn.com/HEALTH/library/ agoraphobia/DS00894.html.

Charles H. Elliott, "Facing Panic Attacks Head On," Psych Central blog, December 13, 2011. http://blogs.psychcentral.com/anxiety /2011/12/facing-panic-attacks-head-on.

Paul Li, "What Happens in the Brain When We Experience a Panic Attack?," *Scientific American*, July 3, 2011. www.scientificamerican.com/ article.cfm?id=what-happens-in-the-brain-when-we-experience.

Mayo Clinic, "Panic Attacks and Panic Disorder," May 31, 2012. www .mayoclinic.com/health/panic-attacks/DS00338.

NIMH, *Panic Disorder: When Fear Overwhelms*, 2010. www.nimh.nih .gov/health/publications/panic-disorder-when-fear-overwhelms /complete-panic-disorder-when-fear-overwhelms.shtml.

Mark Sichel, "The Biochemistry of Panic," HealthyPlace, January 27, 2012. www.healthyplace.com/anxiety-panic/articles/the-biochemist ry-of-panic.

Source Notes

Overview

1. Sara Benincasa, "I Have Panic Attacks," *News* (blog), Frisky, April 14, 2010. www.thefrisky.com.
2. Benincasa, "I Have Panic Attacks."
3. Michael E. Brooks, "A Panic Attack Story," *historymike* (blog), May 1, 2010. http://historymike.blogspot.com.
4. losthighway, "My Long Battle with Panic Disorder and Agoraphobia," Experience Project, March 20, 2010. www.experienceproject.com.
5. John M. Grohol, reviewer, "Panic Disorder Symptoms," Psych Central, June 1, 2010. http://psychcentral.com.
6. Carol W. Berman, *100 Questions & Answers About Panic Disorder*. Sudbury, MA: Jones and Bartlett, 2010, p. 5.
7. Quoted in Stuart Tomlinson, "Troopers Rescue a Former Marine Sniper in Crisis from a Snowy Cascade Forest," *Oregon Live*, February 9, 2012. www.oregonlive.com.
8. Charles H. Elliott, "Facing Panic Attacks Head On," Psych Central blog, December 13, 2011. http://blogs.psychcentral.com.
9. Berman, *100 Questions & Answers About Panic Disorder*, p. 58.
10. RKT, "The Leading Causes of Panic Attacks in the Elderly," *Assisted Living Today*, May 22, 2012. http://assistedlivingtoday.com.
11. Berman, *100 Questions & Answers About Panic Disorder*, p. 25.
12. Massachusetts General Hospital School Psychiatry Program & Madi Resource Center, "Panic Disorder," 2010. www2.massgeneral.org.
13. Anxiety BC, "What Is Panic Disorder?," 2012. www.anxietybc.com.
14. American Psychological Association, "Answers to Your Questions About Panic Disorder," 2012. www.apa.org.
15. Quoted in National Institute of Mental Health, *Panic Disorder: When Fear Overwhelms*, 2010. www.nimh.nih.gov.
16. Quoted in Berman, *100 Questions & Answers About Panic Disorder*, p. v.
17. Mayo Clinic, "Panic Attacks and Panic Disorder," May 31, 2012. www.mayoclinic.com.
18. Peter J. Norton et al., "Smoking Behavior and Alcohol Consumption in Individuals with Panic Attacks," *Journal of Cognitive Psychotherapy*, February 1, 2011. www.ncbi.nlm.nih.gov.
19. Bridges to Recovery, "Panic Disorder—Residential Treatment (FAQs)," 2012. www.bridgestorecovery.com.
20. National Institute of Mental Health, *Panic Disorder*.
21. Benincasa, "I Have Panic Attacks."

What Is Panic Disorder?

22. Ronald L. Hoffman, "The Origin of 'Panic,'" Dr. Ronald Hoffman. www.drhoffman.com/page.cfm/633.
23. Quoted in Thaddeus E. Weckowicz and Helen P. Liebel-Weckowicz, *A History of Great Ideas in Abnormal Psychiatry*. Amsterdam: Elsevier Science, 1990, p. 24.
24. Quoted in Donald F. Klein, "Panic Disorder and Agoraphobia: Hypothesis Hothouse," *Journal of Clinical Psychiatry*, 1996. www.columbia.edu.
25. Klein, "Panic Disorder and Agoraphobia."
26. Klein, "Panic Disorder and Agoraphobia."
27. Berman, *100 Questions & Answers About Panic Disorder*, p. vii.

28. Jason Eric Schiffman, "Panic Attacks: What They Are and How to Stop Them," *Psychology Today*, September 15, 2011. www.psychologytoday.com.

29. Berman, *100 Questions & Answers About Panic Disorder*, p. 43.

30. Jeff Tweedy, "Shaking It Off," *Migraine* (blog), *New York Times*, March 5, 2008. http://migraine.blogs.nytimes.com.

31. Quoted in Margaret Allen, "Out-of-the-Blue Panic Attacks Aren't Without Warning: Data Show Subtle Changes Before Patients Aware of Attack," *SMU Research* (blog), Southern Methodist University, July 26, 2011. http://blog.smu.edu.

32. Quoted in Allen, "Out-of-the-Blue Panic Attacks Aren't Without Warning; Data Show Subtle Changes Before Patients Aware of Attack."

33. Quoted in Allen, "Out-of-the-Blue Panic Attacks Aren't Without Warning; Data Show Subtle Changes Before Patients Aware of Attack."

What Causes Panic Disorder?

34. Brittany, "True Story: I Have Panic Attacks," *Yes and Yes* (blog), January 31, 2011. www.yesandyes.org.

35. Brittany, "True Story."

36. Brittany, "True Story."

37. Brittany, "True Story."

38. Mark Sichel, "The Biochemistry of Panic," HealthyPlace, January 27, 2012. www.healthyplace.com.

39. Benincasa, "I Have Panic Attacks."

40. American Psychological Association, "Answers to Your Questions About Panic Disorder."

41. Quoted in Deborah Brauser, "Stress Causes Slow, Steady Increase in Panic Symptoms," Medscape, June 27, 2011. www.medscape.org.

42. Sichel, "The Biochemistry of Panic."

43. Berman, *100 Questions & Answers About Panic Disorder*, p. 51.

44. Steven J. Seay, "Panic Attack Causes: Fight-or-Flight & the Sympathetic Nervous System," Steven J. Seay, Ph.D., August 11, 2011. www.steveseay.com.

45. Seay, "Panic Attack Causes."

46. Paul Li, "What Happens in the Brain When We Experience a Panic Attack?," *Scientific American*, July 3, 2011. www.scientificamerican.com.

47. Richard Maddock, "Panic Attacks as a Problem of pH," *Scientific American*, May 16, 2010. www.scientificamerican.com.

48. Maddock, "Panic Attacks as a Problem of pH."

What Are the Effects of Panic Disorder?

49. Brooks, "A Panic Attack Story."

50. Brooks, "A Panic Attack Story."

51. losthighway, "My Long Battle with Panic Disorder and Agoraphobia."

52. John Tsilimparis, "Panic About 'Panic,'" Anxiety & Panic Disorder Center of Los Angeles, June 2010. www.panicla.com.

53. Quoted in Berman, *100 Questions & Answers About Panic Disorder*, p. 90.

54. American Psychological Association, "Answers to Your Questions About Panic Disorder."

55. losthighway, "My Long Battle with Panic Disorder and Agoraphobia."

56. losthighway, "My Long Battle with Panic Disorder and Agoraphobia."

57. Quoted in Jan Goodwin, "The VA Health-Care System's Dishonorable Conduct," *Good Housekeeping*, March 2010, p. 5.

58. Quoted in Goodwin, "The VA Health-Care System's Dishonorable Conduct."

59. Brittany, "I Have Panic Attacks."

Can People Overcome Panic Disorder?

60. Anonymous, "Panic Attack: My Personal Hell," *YC Teen*, November/December 2011. www.ycteenmag.org.
61. Anonymous, "Panic Attack."
62. Anonymous, "Panic Attack."
63. Berman, *100 Questions & Answers About Panic Disorder*, p. vii.
64. Ben Martin, "In Depth: Cognitive Behavioral Therapy," Psych Central, 2011. http://psychcentral.com.
65. Berman, *100 Questions & Answers About Panic Disorder*, p. 57.
66. Berman, *100 Questions & Answers About Panic Disorder*, p. 57.
67. American Psychological Association, "Answers to Your Questions About Panic Disorder."
68. Charles H. Elliott, "When Real Panic Flares: Take Direct Action," Psych Central blog, December 13, 2011. http://blogs.psychcentral.com.
69. Malec, Herring, and Krause, "Panic Attacks and Panic Disorder," April 7, 2012. www.malecherringandkrause.com.
70. Martin, "In Depth."
71. Brittany, "I Have Panic Attacks."
72. Mayo Clinic, "Biofeedback," January 26, 2010. www.mayoclinic.com.
73. Jerry Kennard, "'Emotion Ring' Web Trials Look Promising for Panic Disorder," HealthCentral, February 10, 2010. www.healthcentral.com.
74. Brittany, "I Have Panic Attacks."

List of Illustrations

What Is Panic Disorder?
Panic Disorder Rarer than Other Anxiety Disorders   33
Panic Attack Symptoms   34
An Illness of Young Adults   35

What Causes Panic Disorder?
A Complex Interaction   47
Females Have Highest Risk for Panic Disorder   48

What Are the Effects of Panic Disorder?
Panic Disorder Impairs Quality of Life   59
Panic Disorder and Poor Health   60
Familial Risk of Alcohol Abuse   61

Can People Overcome Panic Disorder?
Patients Say Combination Treatment Works Best   73
Therapy Helps Youth Overcome Panic Disorder   74
Hindrances to Treatment Progress   75

Index

Abel, Jennifer L., 31, 69
acrophobia, 25
adolescents. *See* young adults
adrenaline, 40
agoraphobia
    average age of onset of, 35 (graph)
    described, 18, 30, 31
    development of, 18, 52–53, 56
    gender and, 33
    prevalence of, 32, 34
alcohol abuse
    familial risk of, 61 (graph)
    gender and family history of panic
        disorder and, 45
    by men, 16
    prevalence of, 19, 58
American Psychiatric Association, 20
American Psychological Association,
    30
Ankrom, Sheryl, 59
antianxiety medications, 66
antidepressant medications, 66, 72
anxiety as panic trigger, 8
Anxiety BC (support group), 17
anxiety disorders
    effect on quality of life of various,
        50–51
    onset of, average age of, 16, 34, 35
        (graph)
    panic disorder as worst
        manifestation of, 29
    prevalence of various, 16, 33, 33
        (graph)
    suicide and, 54, 58
    types of, 11
Assisted Living Today, 16
asthma, prevalence as comorbid

condition, 32
autonomic nervous system, 40–41

behavioral therapy. *See* cognitive
    behavioral therapy (CBT)
Benincasa, Sara, 10, 21, 37
Beretsky, Summer, 49
Berman, Carol W.
    on agoraphobia as comorbid
        condition, 33
    on conditioning, 64
    on dying from panic attacks, 55
    on GABA system functioning, 40
    on gender of sufferers, 16, 33
    on importance of diagnosis, 29
    on medications, 69, 72
    on prevalence among close
        relatives, 43, 46
    on running away as distraction, 13
    on severest case seen, 14, 16
    on situationally predisposed panic
        attacks, 25
    on sleep and body chemistry, 47
    on treatment success, 63
    on uncued panic attacks, 24
beta blockers, 72
biofeedback, 67
biological malfunction, 17
Bourne, Edmund J., 45
brain
    effect of antidepressant and
        antianxiety medications on, 66
    neurotransmitters, function in,
        39–40
    pH level of, 41–42
    structure of, as contributing factor,
        44, 46

Index

breath, inability to catch, 23, 24
Brooks, Michael E., 11, 49–50
cardiovascular disorders. *See* heart
  disorders
causes. *See* panic disorders
central nervous system, 46
chest pain, 57
children
  depression as comorbid condition
    in, 59
  diagnosis in, 16–17
  effects of panic attacks in, 55
  medications for, 73
  response to panic attacks by, 17
  severe emotional trauma to, as
    contributing factor, 46
chronic fatigue, 26
cognitive behavioral therapy (CBT)
  described, 20, 64, 74 (chart)
  effectiveness of,
    combined with medications, 72,
      73 (graph)
    compared to treatment with
      medications, 66
    as most effective treatment, 71,
      72
  and interoceptive exposure, 64–65
  premise of, 63–64
comorbid conditions, 25–26, 57
  depression, 49, 59
  epilepsy, 32
  heart disorders, 56, 60 (graph), 61
  migraine headaches, 35, 59
  mood disorders, 30
  PTSD, 33 (graph), 35 (graph), 53
  See also agoraphobia; substance
    abuse
conditioning, 64
contributing factors, 8, 17. *See also*
panic disorders.
Cooper, Jason D., 13–14
coronary artery disease. *See* heart

disorders
cued panic attacks, 24–25
death and panic attacks, 55
depression, 26, 47, 59
desensitization exercises, 65
diagnosis
  in children, 16–17
  criteria, 9, 20, 34
  importance of, 29, 58
  medical evaluation, 19
  mental health evaluation, 19–20
*Diagnostic and Statistical Manual
  of Mental Disorders* (American
  Psychiatric Association), 20
dopamine, 40
drug abuse, 16, 58
Dryden-Edwards, Roxanne, 44, 55
dyspnea, 23, 24

effects, 9, 18–19, 56, 58, 59 (chart)
  See also comorbid conditions
elderly, panic attacks in, 16
Elliott, Charles H., 14, 65
emotional anguish as effect, 18–19
environmental factors
  behavior of family members,
    37–38, 48
  major life transitions, 48
  severe emotional stress during
    childhood, 46
  sudden changes in, 16, 44, 45
  See also stress
epilepsy, 32
epinephrine, 40
escape, urge to, 13–14, 40–41
exposure therapy, 64–65

families
  behavior of members in, 37–38, 48
  depression in parents and
    prevalence in, 47
  gender and risk in, 45

prevalence among close relatives of, 17–18, 43, 46

family therapy and youth, 74 (chart)

fear(s)
confronting, as part of therapy, 64–65
cycle of, 18, 26, 30
during panic attacks, described, 49–50
living in constant state of, 19, 52
situationally predisposed panic attacks and, 25

fight or flight response, 13–14, 40–41

Forrest, Jeffrey S., 55

Freud, Sigmund, 23–24

gamma-aminobutyric acid (GABA), 40

gender of sufferers
of agoraphobia as comorbid condition, 33
family history of disorder and, 45
Plato and, 23
female to male rates as to, 16, 32, 48 (chart)

generalized anxiety disorder, 33 (graph), 35 (graph), 50

genetics, 17–18, 43

Ginsberg, David L., 10, 18

Goodwin, Renee D., 58

Gorman, Jack M., 46, 58

Greece, ancient, 22–23

group psychotherapy and youth, 74 (chart)

headaches
migraine, 26, 35, 59
recurrent, 26, 35

heart disorders, 26
age and, 61
prevalence of, 56, 60 (graph)

Hippocrates, 22

history of anxiety, 22–24, 29

Hoffman, Ronald, 22–23

Hollander, Eric, 29, 44, 70

identical twin studies, 17–18

individual psychotherapy and youth, 74 (chart)

inheritance, 17–18, 43

International Association of Anxiety Management, 29

interoceptive exposure, 64–65

in vivo exposure, 65

Journal of Cognitive Psychotherapy, 19

Kennard, Jerry, 67

Klein, Donald F., 24

Komaroff, Anthony, 30, 32, 44

Le Blanc, Raymond, 10

Li, Paul, 41

life experience. *See* environmental factors

Maddock, Richard
on effectiveness of treatments, 70
on genetics as contributing factor, 44
on pH level of brain, 42

Martin, Ben, 64, 66

medications
beta blockers, 72
for children, 73
controversy about use of, 66, 69
effectiveness of
antidepressant, 72
best, 73
combined with CBT, 72, 73 (graph)
speed of, 66
potential to develop dependence

on, 72

Memon, Mohammmed A.
  on brain structure of sufferers, 46
  on comorbid conditions
    asthma and epilepsy, 32
    depression, 59
    heart disease, 56
    mood disorders, 30
    substance abuse, 58
  on effectiveness of treatment, 72
  on panic attack symptoms, 34
Mental Health America, 31
mental illness and suicide, 54
mental illness stigma, 51–52
Meuret, Alicia E., 27–28
migraine headaches, 26, 35, 59
military veterans, prevalence among, 53
Moitra, Ethan, 38–39
mood disorders, 30

nervous system, 40–41, 44, 46
neurotransmitters in brain, 39, 40
nocturnal panic attacks, 24
Norton, Peter J., 19

obsessive-compulsive disorder, 33, 33 (graph), 35 (graph)
100 Questions & Answers About Panic Disorder (Berman), 14, 16

Pan (Greek god), 22–23
panic attacks
  in ancient Greece, 22–23
  conditions often accompanying, 25–26
  cued vs. uncued, 24–25
  described, 8, 11, 36–37, 49–50
  development of agoraphobia as way to avoid, 52
  in the elderly, 16
  frequency of, 56

minutes to peak of, 32
  at night, 24
  panic disorder vs., 14
  situationally bound, 25
  See also symptoms
panic disorder
  contributing factors to, 8, 17
  brain as
    neurotransmitters in, 39–40
    pH level of, 41–42
    structure of, 44, 46
  family environment as, 37–38, 48
  genetics as, 44, 46
  nervous system as, 40–41, 44, 46
  overview of, 47 (illustration)
  severe emotional trauma during childhood as, 46
  stress as, 38–39, 46, 48
  sudden life changes as, 16, 44, 45
  defined, 8
  and risk of heart disease, 61
  signature characteristics of, 24
  trivialized by society, 50, 51–52
parasympathetic nervous system, 41
parental guidance as treatment, 74 (chart)
phobias
  acrophobia, 25
  development of, 58
  simple, 33 (graph)
  social, 35 (graph)
  See also agoraphobia
physical health problems
  as comorbid condition, 60 (graph)
  See also heart disorders
physiological instabilities and uncued panic attacks, 27–28
Plato, 23
post-traumatic stress disorder (PTSD), 33 (graph), 35 (graph), 53
prevalence of panic disorder, 8, 32
  among close relatives, 43, 46

among military veterans, 53
among young adults, 32
and comorbid conditions:
  agoraphobia, 32, 34
  asthma, 32
  heart disorders, 56, 60 (graph)
  substance abuse, 19, 58
and depression in parents of
  sufferers, 47
and severe emotional trauma
  during childhood, 46
and smoking, 19
and substance abuse, 19, 58

Randall, Dave, 14
Reichenberg, Lourie W.
  on agoraphobia, 30
  on CBT as treatment of choice, 71
  on frequency of panic attacks, 56
  on gender and risk in families, 45
relapses, 66, 70
restless leg syndrome, 25
ring biofeedback therapy, 67
Rothbaum, Barbara O., 29, 44, 70

Schiffman, Jason Eric, 22, 25
Seay, Steven J., 40–41
selective serotonin reuptake
  inhibitors, 66, 73
Seligman, Linda
  on agoraphobia, 30
  on CBT as treatment of choice, 71
  on frequency of panic attacks, 56
  on gender and risk in families, 45
separation anxiety, 35 (graph)
serotonin, 40, 66
Sichel, Mark, 37, 39
simple phobia, 35 (graph)
situationally predisposed panic
  attacks, 25
sleep, 47
smoking, 19

social anxiety disorder, prevalence of,
  33 (graph)
social phobia, 35 (graph)
Stein, Dan J., 29, 44, 70
Stevenson, Julie, 10
stigma of mental illness, 51–52
stress
  as contributing factor, 38–39, 48
  as panic trigger, 8
  susceptibility to, 46
  sympathetic nervous system and,
    41
substance abuse
  familial risk of, 61 (graph)
  gender and family history of panic
    disorder and, 45
  by men, 16
  prevalence of, 19, 58
  as result of self-medication, 55
suicide, 54, 58
support groups, 17
sympathetic nervous system, 40–41
symptoms
  average age of onset of, 16, 34, 35
    (graph)
  beta blockers and, 72
  criteria for diagnosis of, 9, 20, 34
  described, 10, 34
  foreshadowing uncued panic
    attacks, 27–28
  as inability to catch breath, 23, 24
  of nocturnal panic attacks, 24
  physical, 13
  suddenness of, 12–13

teenagers. *See* young adults
Timaeus (Plato), 23
Torpy, Janet M., 56
trauma, 44
  PTSD, 33 (graph), 35 (graph), 53
  severe emotional, in children, 46
treatment

biofeedback, 67
effectiveness of, 62, 63, 70, 72, 73
    (graph)
effect of early, 69
failure to seek, 20, 62, 63, 72
hindrances to progress of, 75
    (graph)
informational aspects of, 70
with medications along with
    therapy, 9, 65–66
types of, 20
for young adults, 73, 74 (chart)
See also cognitive behavioral
    therapy (CBT); medications
triggers of panic attacks, 8
absence of, 11, 24–25, 37, 43
identifying, as part of treatment, 64

Tsilimparis, John, 51
Tweedy, Jeff, 26

uncued panic attacks, 24–25, 27–28,
    30

Wemmie, John, 42

YC Teen (online magazine), 62–63
young adults
    onset of panic disorder and, 35
        (graph)
    prevalence of panic disorder in, 32
    response to panic attacks by, 17
    substance abuse and, 55
    treatment of, 73, 74 (chart)

About the Author

Peggy J. Parks holds a bachelor of science degree from Aquinas College in Grand Rapids, Michigan, where she graduated magna cum laude. An author who has written more than one hundred educational books for children and young adults, Parks lives in Muskegon, Michigan, a town that she says inspires her writing because of its location on the shores of Lake Michigan.